ENNEAGRAM POP!
FICTIONAL CHARACTERS

Damian Hospital and Tony Vahl

All Hasbro, Marvel, DC, Star Trek, Star Wars, Fox, WB, Disney, and other copyrighted characters and the distinctive likeness(es) thereof are Trademarks & Copyright to their respective owners. ALL RIGHTS RESERVED.

Copyright Disclaimer under section 107 of the Copyright Act 1976, allowance is made for "fair use" for purposes such as non-fiction criticism, comment, news reporting, teaching, scholarship, education and research. Fair use is a use permitted by copyright statute that might otherwise be infringing.

Copyright 2013 ꙮ Tony Vahl and Damian Hospital

All rights reserved.

ISBN: 1482624648
ISBN-13: 978-1482624649

No part of this publication may be reproduced, distributed, or transmitted in any form or by any means, including photocopying, recording, or other electronic or mechanical methods, without the prior written permission of the publisher, except in the case of brief quotations embodied in critical reviews and certain other noncommercial uses permitted by copyright law. For permission requests, write to the publisher at numbersix@dailyskew.com.

Published in the United States of America.

Cover design: Damian Hospital

Edited by: Tony Vahl and Damian Hospital

Published by: The DailySkew
dailyskew.com

Version 2013.8.26

Tony Vahl and Damian Hospital

Enneagram Pop! Series:

Visit Enneagrampop.com to leave feedback, listen to audio, learn more about the enneagram, and updates for the latest Enneagram Pop! series.

Dedicated to Destiny, who guided Damian and Tony to the Enneagram, with special thanks to Dr. Richard Hoffman and Amanda Hoffman.

More special thanks: to Amazon for creating the Kindle platform for authors, to Candelabrum for making command line operations user-friendly, and Google for making document collaboration ridiculously easy.

Introduction

Introduction

If you're reading this book, you probably know a thing or two ... or nine ... about the Enneagram. However, for those of you who are uninitiated, here is a brief explanation of what the Enneagram is, from our dailyskew.com Enneagram Primer page:

Understanding the Enneagram is like swallowing the red pill that allows you to escape the Matrix.

Once you've soaked in the details of the nine personality types, you'll almost expect to wake up with Morpheus standing over you, saying, "Welcome ... to the real world."

The Enneagram is not about labeling; it's not about what type you are -- what personality traits you're stuck with.

The Enneagram is about escaping the fear-controlled boundaries we've set for ourselves. It's about letting go of our habitual defenses, and understanding that we don't need them to survive.

The Enneagram is about seeing the world as it really is -- removing our biased, preconceived notions, and opening our eyes to the real truth. The Enneagram is about breaking the cycle that keeps us from achieving our greatest desire.

Pretty deep, huh?

For more detailed information about the Enneagram, you can read Personality Types by Riso and Hudson. Damian and I read this book in 1999, and our lives were forever changed by the knowledge contained in those pages.

For now, just understand that the Enneagram is like the Briggs-Myers personality test, except there are 9 basic personality types, where there are 16 possibilities with Briggs-Myers. Here is a list of each personality type, with a link to the description on the Enneagram Institute website (the online home for the authors of the book Personality Types). Please click each link and read the descriptions there for a summary of each type:

Type 1: The Reformer

Type 2: The Helper

Type 3: The Achiever

Type 4: The Individualist

Type 5: The Investigator

Type 6: The Loyalist

Type 7: The Enthusiast

Type 8: The Challenger

Type 9: The Peacemaker

In each chapter, we will present three examples of a personality type, with detailed analysis: one unhealthy individual, one average, and one healthy. Each analysis will be followed by a brief list of other characters who fall under that particular personality type and range of healthiness, with a brief description for each.

Oh, and you will see mention of "Wings." What are wings in an Enneagram context? To answer that question, let's take a look at a public domain picture of the Enneagram symbol, from Wikipedia:

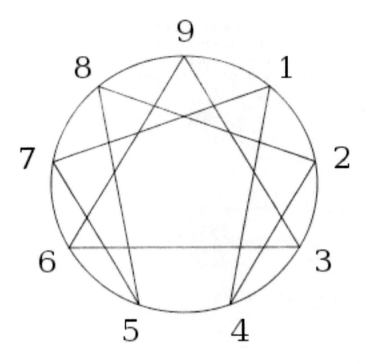

As you can see, there are nine types positioned on a circle, interconnected by lines. Each type has a number to the left and right. For example, Type 9 has 8 on one side, and 1 on the other. For Type 9, 8 and 1 are possible wings. You could have a Type 9 with an 8 wing, or a Type 9 with a 1 wing. The wing is a compliment to the core personality type, and depending on how strong the wing is, can create a subtype personality. A 9 with a distinct 8 wing can be referred to as a 9w8, and a 9 with a 1 wing can be called a 9w1. The 9 remains the dominant personality, but the wing can alter the personality.

Confused? If you are new to the Enneagram, I seriously recommend reading Personality Types. You will get far more out of this book if you have a basic understanding of the Enneagram first. At the very least, read about the personality types on the Enneagram Institute website first.

Anyway, just relax and have some fun reading this book. In learning about the hidden motivations for each character listed, you might learn something useful about yourself and the people around you. Entertainment and education: what a concept!

Definitions:

Fear/Desires: *The core belief of the person.*
Motivations: *The core belief put into action.*
Important Life Events: *Brief history.*
Reactions Under Stress: *How the character reveals personality under fire.*
Mental Health Range: *Healthy (1-3), Average (4-6), Unhealthy (7-9), with 1 being enlightened, and 9 being at rock bottom. These numbers are NOT personality types, they are the Levels of Development.*
The Wing Slider: *Every type is influenced by its two nearest types in the Enneagram, such as 2w3 or 2w1. The wing may be strong, weak, balanced, or close to none, i.e a "straight 2" means no wing.*
Instinctive Subtype: *Self-Preservation, Social, or Sexual- pretty self-explanatory.*
Quirks: *Subjective patterns that the authors have seen with types, including similar quotes or physical traits.*
Also Could Be: *In all fairness, the authors are giving their "best guess", so this section offers alternative possibilities.*

HOW TO TYPE YOURSELF

How to Type Yourself
As mentioned in the Introduction, if you are new to the Enneagram, you should consider reading the bible for Enneagram aficionados, Personality Types by Riso and Hudson. One reason you should do so is to know your type.

Using the book Personality Types, you can figure out your type fairly quickly. In order to utilize this chapter, you will need the print or ebook edition of Personality Types. Once you have the book in hand, here are the steps we've used in the past that can help you find your type:

Step 1:
If you have the physical book, look at the back cover. If you have the Kindle ebook, go to location 762, which is in chapter 3. If you do not have the book, you can view the descriptions for each type at the EnneagramInstitute.com website.

Read through the four-word descriptions for each personality type. As you read, look for the description that clicks with you, that describes you the best, that you relate to the most. It is possible that multiple descriptions will appeal to you. This is okay. As you learn more about the Enneagram, this will actually make sense in most cases.

Step 2:
Once you've found the type or types that click with you the most, turn to the Appendix and flip to the section about Core Dynamics, and keep going until you get to the diagrams for each type. In the ebook, this is location 8382. There is no online equivalent available for free at the

EnneagramInstitute.com site. You can read through the expanded definitions for each type, but it's not the same as reading through the Core Dynamics first.

Flip ahead to the type or types you chose in Step 1. Read through each diagram, starting on the right-side of level 1 with Basic Fear, follow the arrow down to level 2 and Basic Desire, and then follow the arrow up to level 1 and Self-Actualization. Then follow the arrows to read the A-Terms and B-Terms for level 1. Continue reading this way for all 9 levels of development.

As you read through the levels of development for your type, it should feel like a biography about yourself. Every descriptive word should hit you to the core. You might feel compelled to turn away, it's so accurate. That's okay. Learning that the Matrix is an illusion is a tough experience for anyone whose mind has been freed.

Some of you, in order to compensate for this feeling of being punched in the gut, will choose to relate to a personality type you want to be. For example, Damian and I were close friends with a co-worker who we both agreed was a Type 7, yet when introduced to Personality Types, he decided that he was a Type 4. He related to the core dynamics of the Individualist because that is what he wanted to be, not because that was what he was. Be careful, as you might make the same mistake. After awhile, if you notice that the type you chose does not seem to click with you, repeat steps 1 and 2 until you find your true personality type.

Step 3:

If you have the Personality Types book, go to Part II of the book, find the chapter about your type and read it. You should feel a confirmation that the type you chose is correct as you read through Profile, Overview, and Analysis of the Levels of Development.

Alternate method for discovering your personality type:

If you are unable to find your type using the method above, consider taking the RHETI test on the EnneagramInstitute.com website. The full version of the test is $10 as of this writing, and there is a free sample of the RHETI test available. The free sample should get you in the ballpark, so to speak, and the $10 version version is available if you need more accurate results.

If, after following these steps, you still can't find a personality type that "clicks", the Enneagram Personality Type system is probably not for you. That's fine. You probably have a strong wing or are so enlightened (or unhealthy) that you have integrated (or disintegrated) into another type. If you want something more fixed and less dynamic, try the Myers Briggs Personality Test instead, or study Carl Jung's four streams of consciousness and extroversion vs introversion attitudes.

Part One
Type 1

The Baroness

As mentioned in the introduction, you can split each personality into three categories: unhealthy, average, and healthy. Each category speaks for itself, describing how people express their personality type. If the person is acting out in an unhealthy manner, they have succumbed to their basic fears and are on the path to self-destruction. If he or she is healthy, the best qualities of that person shine through, and the person incorporates good qualities from other types. Average is just that: middle of the road, neither hot nor cold, kind of beat-bopping through life.

We will start with a look at an unhealthy Type 1 fictional character, and follow that with a list and brief descriptions of other unhealthy Type 1's.

A.k.a. Anastasia DeCobray, the Baroness is a villain from the G.I. Joe universe of characters. How do we know she is a Type 1?

Fear/Desires: She has a skewed sense of justice, and must be correct; afraid of being wrong and death.
Motivations: To avenge the death of her brother; to make America pay.
Important Life Events: Death of her brother, joins Cobra Command, meets Destro, runs Cobra by manipulating Cobra Commander II, retires with Destro for a while.

Reactions Under Stress: Will kill, switch alliances, and make deals.
Mental Health Range: Average 4 down to Unhealthy 9
The Wing Slider: Very strong 1w2
Instinctive Subtype: Sexual
Quirks: Physically looks like a One librarian with a fetish outfit. Snobby, rich, aristocrat.
Also Could Be: Could be a type 8 due to her need to control and her ruthless nature, but she is more subtle than traditional Eights. In terms of power, Eights don't "bide their time" to lead or to go renegade- they "just do it" and generally seize it very transparently. Eights are highly expressive in relationships, rarely surrender, and don't retire in their primes. It's possible the modern IDW version of The Baroness has Eight traits, but most of her characterization comes from Marvel Comics and the cartoons, where she is subtle and manipulative behind-the-scenes. Let's put it another way way: The Incredible Hulk is an unhealthy Eight: a wild brute who is direct and who can't contain his emotions. **There is a very small chance she is a Type 5 due to her coldness, but Fives don't have the drive for vengeance or acting skills like she does.**

COBRA
INTELLIGENCE OFFICER
Code Name: BARONESS

Primary Military Specialty: Intelligence
Secondary Military Specialty: Fixed Wing Pilot
Birthplace: Classified

The spoiled offspring of wealthy European aristocrats, tl Baroness graduated from student radicalism into intern tional terrorism and finally into the ranks of COBRA. Sl was severely burned during a COBRA night attack operatic and has had extensive plastic surgery. Rumor has it that sl is the only one who knows Destro's secret identity. Qualifi expert: M-16; AK-47; RPG7; Uzi; H.I.S.S. tank operator.

"Her principal weakness is in the division of her loyal between COBRA Commander and Destro. Her chief streng would seem to lie in her ability to play them against ea other."

Copyright © 1982 Hasbro ALL RIGHTS RESERVED

The Baroness is a villain, to be sure, but she was not born bad. In Marvel Comics, The Baroness' motivation is to avenge the alleged death of her brother. Along the way, she becomes a principled terrorist, with a mission to stop US foreign policy. She thinks she's right. She's not running a money scam, like the Cobra Commander does. The Baroness is dominant, who manipulates others under the illusion of being submissive or as an adviser. She engages in extreme emotional cruelty. This Unhealthy Type 1 also has a strong, yet hypocritical, belief system.

The existence of the Baroness's brother was part of a later storyline in Marvel's G.I. JOE 93 and not mentioned afterwards when Devil's Due and IDW published the series, nor has it been featured in any cartoons. So, for the bulk of The Baroness' appearances her motivations may seem to be as a stock villain. But for those readers who read that secret origin, it was a good reward.

The Baroness is the European spy archetype: undercover, deceitful, able to sleep and manipulate unsuspecting men to extract information for her bosses. The Type 1 female spy is very efficient because of her pure logic, patience, and cold rationale. Although the Baroness' anti-American revolutionary operations put her at extreme risk in the field, the Baroness does not hesitate to surrender when the odds are not in her favor. Her 1982 action figure file card shows that she's a snobby aristocrat. This is also a key trait of some wealthy Type 1's (nose in the air).

The generic female Type 1 is a schoolteacher, a religious instructor, a strict office manager, or lawyer. The Baroness is like a prosecutor. She becomes a terrorist and spy after she had determined that the US was a hypocritical, imperialist nation that lied about its foreign policy. So, she supports anti-American revolutionary rebel groups all around the world. All of this is revealed through flashbacks in the aforementioned G.I. JOE 93-96.

Written by the legendary Larry Hama, who effectively created the character, it is revealed that she was a square when she was younger, but she had flipped out when she saw her brother getting shot. She wrongly blames Snake Eyes for his death. (It had turned out that her brother survived, and Snake Eyes was innocent in the scene.) She dedicates her entire life to get the intel as to where to locate the perceived assassin and make him suffer beyond words, and part of this is teaming with unsavory characters. In other words, she compromises her belief system because the emotions of loss and vengeance overtake her logic.

Her only true love is Destro, who is a romantic Enneagram Type 4. Destro was present when her brother was shot, and has always been there to support The Baroness emotionally. Although the Baroness uses sex appeal to manipulate men, she's extremely picky and perfectionistic regarding who she chooses to open up to. You can imagine how frustrating this is for guys or gals who love unhealthy female Ones. I mean, she's extremely picky, yet she sleeps around! Geez.

Even though she loves Destro, at times the relationship is very one-sided. Destro worships her while she likes to focus on the more practical terms of the relationship. She keeps him at a distance. She still uses her body to advance her career or help her skewed cause, while Destro seems a little more loyal, in that regard. Other types give into the passion.

The 1 is the exact opposite of the 2, the Helper, especially the female versions. The typical 2 is the generic mother: loving, nurturing, caring, and emotional. The female 1 is cold, calculating, punishing, strict, distant, and really doesn't express love easily.

That's why the wings, 1w2 or 2w1, create such a conflicted and contradictory personality. The Baroness is probably a 1w2 more than a 1w9, and she's psychotic sometimes. In some later Marvel comics (69+), the Baroness actually reforms and settles down with Destro. This also shows she's probably a 1w2, by tapping into that 2 wing.

Other 1's are just too robotic, like Sinestro from the Green Lantern comics. We would say the Baroness' 2 wing also attributes to her sexual passion she has with Destro, and some of her shocking sacrifices she makes for him, later on in the comics (120+).

Reformation and self-improvement are major goals for the Enneagram Type 1. Although modern day comics brought the Baroness back to her roots as the evil spy, her nature is to grow, since she began the path of evil under false pretenses.

Unfortunately, The Baroness reverts back to a straight Cobra villain working for Cobra Commander at the end of the Marvel series, and this continues with the other publishers. Perhaps even more disappointing is that IDW rebooted the universe and created a new origin for her in ORIGINS 12+. In the revised origin, she just got bored being a rich girl and joins a terrorist group called The Red Hand and falls in love with its leader. Therefore for new fans who had never picked up the obscure Marvel origin issues, her motivation seems one-dimensional or whimsical. However it still fits with being a Type One when it comes to being a snobby little poor rich girl using her looks to cause trouble.

We have been typing characters and people since 1999, and it is a subjective and instinctive process; even surveys and polls can be misleading.One of the ways to type people is by looks, but it is not recommended at all. Let's start with a brief history of personality: in the 1950's, psychologists used physical appearance as a basis for personality types, such as the concepts of endomorphism and ectomorphism, which says, pretty much, that fat people are lazy, and skinny people are energetic. Obviously, it's not significantly proven by statistics or studies, and even if it happens to be true, there are way too many exceptions to make that system practical for judgments.

With the Enneagram, physical appearance is not reliable, but it is circumstantial evidence for when we begin to type someone. Sometimes the voice, mannerisms, or fashion sense can be signs of a particular type. Even phrases can indicate an Enneagram Type.

Again, it's just the initial sensory input we receive. We use deductive reasoning, like Sherlock Holmes, or Fox Mulder, or Dr. House. If you try to type everyone on looks, you're going to be on the wrong track.

A common example of mistyping people comes from from the world of politics: John McCain. Many websites such as ashlandenneagram.com, davesenneagram.com, everydayenneagramblog.blogspot.com, and many others list McCain as the gruff old Type 8, mostly based on his looks, mannerisms, and bursts of anger. McCain gets grouped with older outspoken angry men like Bill

O'Reilly, Donald Trump, George Steinbrenner, and others, but based on his background (and younger self) we feel he's really a Type 4 The point is that people can project some physical similarities but it doesn't necessarily mean they are in the same group. We have to dig deeper under the surface.

All of that said, The Baroness looks like a Type 1, and it turns out she is a 1! Comparing people's quirks from those whom one meets in life is a valuable frame of reference if one wants to type characters, other people, or themselves. In Damian's life, he knew two female co-workers that had The Baroness's facial features, the predominant glasses, the jet-black hair, the pale skin, and the petite body. Ironically, they both had the same first name. The women (and The Baroness) were involved in the drama of a love triangle (separate, and not involving Damian). They had the ability to turn off their emotions under stressful and intimate situations. This is a skill that most types do not have (Nines can do it easily).

Another One who has the fetish outfit style (and is a spy) is Black Widow from Marvel Comics; she also found herself in a love triangle (as did The Baroness with Cobra Commander and Destro) in the 1980s with Hawkeye and Daredevil. Ursa from the movie Superman II also has an S&M image and has a cold, cruel, yet flirtatious personality.

What we've learned:
- Female Ones are hot-and-cold to the extreme in relationships.
- They may enjoy role-playing.
- Unhealthy Ones are extremely cruel and inhuman.
- Ones are influenced by belief systems and philosophies. and rationalize the breaking of rules.
- Typing characters or people based on physical appearance is a risky business, but such clues should not be ignored totally as they can be valuable in making a final determination.

Other Unhealthy 1's
Agent Smith
Agent Smith [Matrix movies] is a symbol of U.S. government agents, which in turn represent order, bureaucracy, the law, and the enforcement of law- no exceptions, no breaks, cold, and unrelenting. As the trilogy progressed, he went from maintaining the status quo to desiring to kill all humans and machines. Deep down, he desired freedom, and eventually made the choice to disobey and stay in the Matrix after being defeated by Neo. Eventually he learned to duplicate himself, spreading through the Matrix like a virus, and even reaching the real world to attack his enemies. Unlike 8's, Smith displays control over his emotions, as well as a sinister logic when acting out his murderous plans.

Sinestro
Sinestro [DC Comics] strives for order and perfection to the extreme, to the point of a willingness to commit murder to achieve order. He enjoys punishing others and is dominant. Sinestro is obsessive compulsive, strict, cold-hearted, dangerous. After becoming the greatest Green Lantern of them all and a teacher, he abuses his power and is punished by the Guardians. He ends up creating a yellow ring to fight the GLC. Some time later, he somewhat reforms, teams with former enemies to battle a greater evil, and becomes a Green Lantern again. Like other 1's, he can be like a snobby dictator, complete with a distinctive mustache.

Tri-Klops

Tri-Klops [Masters of the Universe] is a Type One who has accepted his role as being Skeletor's underling. An expert swordsman and builder, he is Skeletor's tech go-to man. He rivals Man-At-Arms' inventions. Tri-Klops is pragmatically loyal to Skeletor as opposed to emotionally loyal- his duty comes from logic. He becomes cowardly and subservient when under stress. He is a prototypical engineer. Tri-Klops acts like a defeated samurai at times, and is also hypocritical. He uses his new vision to spy on others. He is Man-At-Arms' "opposite," who also happens to be a Type 1. Tri-Klops may also be a Type 6; Masters of the Universe doesn't characterize Skeletor's underlings very well.

Vigilante

The Vigilante [DC Comics] was a frustrated prosecutor who decided to take the law in his own hands. Motivated by the death of his family at the hands of mobsters, Adrian Chase was consumed by his determination to rid the streets of injustice. Trained by vengeance spirits, his downward spiral began when he allowed a cop to die. He was hunted down by authorities, quit, then killed his friend who assumed the Vigilante identity. Ultimately, his inner demons led to his suicide. Chase was dominated by fear of loss; fear is a very influential emotion for Ones. His professions were lawyer and judge, which are symbols of the Law, the main representation of Ones.

Brainiac

Brainiac [DC Comics] is a typical robot Type 1: cold, calculating, and logical. Part of being a supercomputer is to look down upon all organic things; the fact that he prefers green skin or metallic features to typical human skin color demonstrates that he is detached from humanity and other biological life forms. Brainiac has evolved more and more into a computer than when he first appeared, in which he was originally an ambitious collector and destroyer. As a typical One, Brainiac likes to think he doesn't have an ego, but he does. Over the years, he has shrunk cities to collect them and fought Superman. He could also be a Type 5, like Luthor. Both unhealthy 1's and unhealthy 5's are completely detached from reality.

Ursa

Ursa [DC Comics] looks like an S&M One (fetish outfit, black hair, pale skin). She is cruel, cold-hearted, and completely unlikable. She only has a passion for General Zod and torturing others. The imprisonment in the Phantom Zone by the Kryptonian High Council only served to make her even more detached from other beings. She has a definite air of superiority. Ursa has a strong 2-wing, as exhibited by her loyalty to Zod, and motherly attitude towards Nog. She could be a Darth Vader 9 who loyally follows her master. Not much is known about her. In the older comics, the core of the character is the same: a cruel woman who is loyal to Zod only.

Raymond Barone

Ray Barone is a New York Sportswriter who is married with three children. His parents and older brother live across the street. He lives in fear of his mother, and will do anything to maintain his status as mama's boy, even taking her side when she disagrees with his wife, Debra. Incredibly insensitive to his wife's needs, and the needs of his children. Values golf more than spending time with the family.

Padme Amidala

You will find there tend to be more average people or characters in this book than unhealthy or healthy. We suppose it corresponds with some cosmic Bell Curve, where the majority tend to be somewhere in the middle, and outliers live on the short right or left ends of the curve.

Let's take a look at a great example of an average Type 1 fictional character, Padme Amidala, followed by a list of other average Type 1's.

Fear/Desires: To maintain order.
Motivations: Strives to maintain the Republic and bring peace to the galaxy through politics.
Important Life Events: As Queen of the Naboo, successfully repelled a droid invasion army, while uniting her people with the underwater Gungans. Elected Senator from Naboo. Marries Anakin Skywalker in secret. Gives birth to Luke and Leia before dying.
Reactions Under Stress: A fighter who, in the end, gave up on life when her husband became evil and attacked her.
Mental Health Range: 3-7. Seems healthy at times, but there are holes in her game, like when she snuck off and married Anakin, knowing full-well that was against Jedi rules.
The Wing Slider: Active 2-wing.
Instinctive Subtype: Self-Preservation.
Quirks: Very orderly wardrobe, hot and cold love life, chooses only

one man, dark hair, pale skin, professional, tough.

Also Could Be: Star Wars characters can be hard to type, at times. George Lucas appears to be a Type 6, and injects his personality into each character. We're pretty sure Amidala is a 1, but she could be a peacemaker Type 9.

© 2002, Lucasfilm Ltd. All Rights Reserved.

Padmé Amidala is best known as being the wife of Anakin Skywalker (who later becomes Darth Vader). Her story is told in Star Wars I-III, also called the Prequel Trilogy. She was created by George Lucas. Her main function in Star Wars mythology is to be the catalyst for Anakin to go crazy and become a villain. Her secondary function is the political plot that enables Senator Palpatine to rule. Interestingly enough, although she is supposed to be an archetype for wisdom, she makes two costly mistakes in judgement.

She contrasts her husband well. She is ethical, has a strong sense of right and wrong, and advocates for positive change and improvement in the Republic. However, she is not aggressive in politics, as she defaults to Senator Palpatine's misleading advice and leadership. Palpatine manipulates her and takes over the galaxy due to her peaceful nature and lack of instincts.

Padmé Amidala is a 1w2. Half of her is logical, professional, and business-like. The other half is an earth-mother: compassionate, sympathetic, and loving woman. She gave her heart to one man: Anakin Skywalker. That's a trait of many 1w2's: they love one person deeply, sometimes once in their entire life.

Her passion is politics and working with the senate. Padmé displays the reformer key component of being a 1. She wants peace within the Republic, while Palpatine is revealed to be a war-monger. She is protective of her home Naboo (Naboo is actually an ancient word for wisdom. He was the god of wisdom from ancient Mesopotamia. Type Ones are associated with wisdom.) Until Anakin came along, that seemed to be her only priority. Like many Ones, she is a workaholic and does not seek out romance.

Yet Anakin is aggressive with her. She would never have made the first move with him. In fact, she had viewed Anakin as a little boy, because that is who he was when she first met him. So, it is very possible she would have remained professional and cold in terms of having a relationship with anyone, until Anakin comes along and is very melodramatic in wooing her.

The reason why she is an average One is because she didn't handle the relationship as ideally as she could have. She was young, and she was still learning about the world. Unfortunately, her life was cut short, thanks to her husband. Ultimately, she didn't see the signs that Anakin was mentally unstable. She was a little too lenient, even though all the evidence was there regarding him turning to the dark side and doing things that she would not have approved of.

Anakin broke her heart. That broken heart went all the way to the delivery room, when she gave up on life after the birth of her two children, Luke and Leia Skywalker. She was consumed by fear and she had no desire to live out the rest of her life. That's why we don't rate her as being healthy: the traumatic experience of betrayal was too much for her and she lost her desire to live.

Padmé is not a damsel in distress. She is very tough and assertive. Unfortunately, her undoing is her gullibility and trust in not only Anakin, but also Senator/Chancellor Palpatine, who later becomes Emperor Palpatine. Padmé is a tragic hero. Her noble spirit lives on in her two children. A lot of her can be seen in Princess Leia, her famous daughter in the Original Trilogy.

Ones are not the most instinctive types. They are by-the-book and compliant when it comes to rules and regulations. Don't get us wrong: some 1's are rebellious and do fight back. She does, but it's just too late, as Palpatine took over. She didn't have the full awareness of what was going on with her husband or the senate.

Padmé is a great example of a female Type 1 who has a loving edge to her, which is the 1w2 subtype. Like many 1's, Padmé evolves and grows. You can actually see this in her physical appearance, when you compare how she looks from Star Wars Episodes I through III.

George Lucas was shooting for Padmé Amidala to represent wisdom from Naboo, in addition to the type 2 female earth-goddess, who is capable of unlimited compassion. Padmé forgives Anakin, even when he had confessed his sins to her on Tatooine. On the lava planet Mustafar she gives him the benefit of the doubt, even after Obi-Wan Kenobi told her everything that he did, including the senseless murder of the younglings, who were Jedis in training.

What we've learned:
- Ones are professional, serious, and workaholics.
- Ones are capable of great wisdom, but may be blinded by their love or obedience to an authority figure.
- A 1w2 is more expressive than straight Ones or 1w9s.
- Although you may not think Padmé and The Baroness (the unhealthy One from G.I. JOE) are similar due to one being evil and one being good, as well as being from different settings, they are both 1w2s. They both believe that they are righteous. They act hot-and-cold to their one lover, have issues in relationships, are out of touch with their instincts, are not damsels in distress, are intelligent, do things that can be considered hypocritical, and actually share some physical characteristics

(thin, pale skin, dark hair, short).
- A character can be totally good, compassionate, beautiful, and heroic, but still not healthy on the Enneagram level of development scale. The majority of all characters in fiction have some flaw in them, as apparently enlightened characters are deemed boring by the public.

Other Average 1's
Time Variance Authority

The Time Variance Authority [Marvel Comics] is an extra dimensional bureaucracy that manages and audits timelines. The TVA was based upon Marvel's editorial structure at the time. In particular, middle management bureaucrat Mobius M. Mobius was based on Mark Gruenwald, who was a well-known writer/editor for Marvel, and a keeper of continuity within the crazy Marvel bullpen of the 1980's. In addition, the initials are a homage to the U.S. government's Tennessee Valley Authority. They attempted to punish the Fantastic Four for breaking time-travel rules. Ultimately, the TVA is a symbol of all paper heavy, detailed oriented, and cold-hearted bureaucracies, such as the IRS or law firms, which is symbolic of Type 1's. Also, like your typical government bureaucracy, there are limits to the TVA's jurisdiction that they are not likely to admit.

T'Pol

T'Pol [Star Trek] is pretty much a female version of Mr. Spock, except she is 100% Vulcan and even more cold. She was the first Vulcan to serve aboard a starship with humans for an extended time. Her basic physical features are in line with other Type Ones that the DailySkew.com has E-grammed. Like The Baroness, she was once a spy. T'Pol has struggled with controlling her emotions, and has learned from her experiences serving on the Enterprise with Captain Archer.

Man-at-Arms
Man-at-Arms, a.k.a. Duncan, [Masters of the Universe] is He-Man's mentor and teacher. He is a master strategist, mechanic, and designer. He prefers finding alternatives to direct combat. As mentioned earlier, Masters of the Universe tended to create good and evil opposites to simplify things; his opposite is Tri-Klops. The Filmation crew decided to give him the distinctive mustache, which is common amongst male Type Ones. Man-at-Arms thinks with his head, not with his emotions. His one weakness is his love for his daughter, Teela.

Lois Lane
Lois Lane [DC Comics] is a truth seeker, and strives to create social reform and justice via investigative journalism. She does everything on principle, is an advocate, doesn't follow orders, and is hyper-critical. Throughout her long history, she has always been a tough-as-nails reporter. Lois was married to Superman prior to the DC New 52 reboot, and her Earth-2 counterpart was also married to the Man of Steel. Ultimately, Superman chose the most "perfect" woman to give his heart to.

Walter Skinner
Walter Skinner [X-Files] is an FBI Assistant Director who tries to play things by the book. Originally at odds with Fox Mulder over the X-Files, he eventually came around to Mulder's way of thinking. He respects protocol, chain of command, and complies with "upper management". That being said, he eventually shows that his quest for justice is more important than rules and regulations (he couldn't stand feeling guilty about cover-ups and deaths by the U.S. government).

Debra Barone
Debra is the embattled wife of Ray Barone, and the mother of their three children. She attempts to create a family atmosphere, in spite of Ray's lack of participation and the constant interference from the in-laws. Debra is constantly having to battle Marie, Ray's mom, over family issues, like her cooking or how to raise the kids, or how to treat Ray. Since she rarely gets moral support from her husband, Debra is reduced to yelling at him, or yelling at Marie, or storming off upstairs. Her

attempts at creating a perfect family are constantly thwarted. Even when she attempted to find an ally in her battle against Marie, her best friend Amy, Ray went to his parents and told them everything. Marie came in and quickly ruined her plans. If she were a healthy type 1, she would have divorced Ray a long time ago.

Spock

Now let's turn to an exceptional example of a healthy Type One reformer: Mr. Spock. Following his profile will be a couple of more examples of healthy 1's. Remember that most characters in this book will fall in the average range of development. Truly healthy, self-actualized characters in fiction are rare.

Fear/Desires: Spock fears giving into his human emotions and passions.
Motivations: To get the respect of his father, to save the universe, to be right.
Important Life Events: Conflicts with father, being bullied as a kid for being half-human, joining Starfleet instead of a traditional Vulcan role, befriending Captain Kirk, becoming the most competent officer, sacrificing himself, being reborn and more at ease with himself.
Reactions Under Stress: Plans a solution.
Mental Health Range: 1-6, he is a strong healthy character but sometimes his character is too critical and unforgiving so the writers could create drama.
The Wing Slider: Straight One.
Instinctive Subtype: Self-preservation.
Quirks: Being mocked by Dr. McCoy for being a computer, keeping the same expression.
Also Could Be: Nope. Spock is the perfect example of a One, and all

Ones can relate to him.

January 12, 1968 NBC Television press release photo

Mr. Spock from Star Trek may be the most obvious and famous Healthy One in entertainment. Most Americans can instantly recognize Spock, but more importantly they understand how unique his personality is: he is pure logic, but has a human side to him that he tries to suppress. Of all the various memorable and deep Star Trek characters, none can approach the legacy of Spock.

Like all Ones, Spock has to be right. The difference between Spock and an Average One is that Spock is actually right most of, if not all the time. He has a computer-like genius, can easily master any subject matter, lives a Spartan existence, follows all of Starfleet's rules and regulations, and he enjoys philosophical debates while respecting Vulcan traditions.

Spock's inner conflict is that he is half-Vulcan/half-human. Vulcans suppress their emotions, as they deem them illogical and impracticable. Spock is secretly self-loathing and embarrassed by his human side because it's not really accepted in Vulcan society. However he does love his mother, and appreciates her unconditional love, while his father Sarek is more cold, strict, and critical. As a One, Spock has a rebellious spirit, and goes against his father's wishes and generally is portrayed as a loner. Much of Spock's upbringing and relationship with his parents are mentioned in the Star Trek Original Series episode "Journey to Babel", and The Animated Series episode "Yesteryear". The new 2009 Star Trek feature film, which introduces a new version of Spock, keeps his origin intact and validates "Yesteryear".

Spock's Vulcan race can also be considered as a One as well, and generally their society is depicted as being repressed and harsh- especially all of their appearances in the Enterprise series. It's also one reason why fans view other Vulcan crew members in later series as "copies of Spock".

Although Spock is an alien, ironically his inner turmoil is exactly what Type Ones goes through: Ones are self-critical perfectionists, and don't like to express their needs or emotions. Ones are generally frugal and self-denying martyrs.

Spock is the logical and technical component of the triad that runs the Enterprise in the original Star Trek series: Captain Kirk (Type 7) is the leader, decision maker, and risk taker; Doctor McCoy (Type 2) is the emotional and compassionate one. It is a mirror of Sigmund Freud's concept of Ego (Kirk), Super Ego (Spock), and Id (McCoy). Both Spock and McCoy offer advice to Kirk, and as the leader he would weigh both sides and make his own decision, taking full responsibility.

Healthy Ones willingly sacrifice themselves to save lives, and Spock practiced what he preached- "The needs of the many outweigh the needs of the one"- when he dies to save the crew in the Star Trek: The Wrath of Khan movie.

Spock is solidly healthy, but the writers continually have him debate, nitpick, suppress his emotions, and act cold; definitely average traits. However, over the years- especially after his death and resurrection- Spock has become at ease with himself, no longer has the need to live in the shadow of Sarek, and actually expresses his feelings in the motion pictures and his appearances in The Next Generation ("Unification"). Therefore, the 1960s Spock is slightly less healthy than the 1980s and beyond version, but only because the writers needed to create drama and conflict, not because of his actions or philosophies.

The new version of Spock (who is younger) seems to have a head start on coming to terms with who he is because the original Spock gave him advice. Ones in fiction fulfill the function of being mentors. Joseph Campbell's hero's journey story theory has a role for the wise old teacher, and Spock becomes that in the new movie.

If you are just learning about the Enneagram or have begun typing people and characters on your own, feel free to use Spock as the best and clearest example of an Enneagram Type 1, and compare others to him.

What we've learned:
- Ones have inner conflicts concerning their emotions, and don't like to express them. Healthy Ones have the ability to come to terms with them and express them in a natural way.
- Spock is the perfect example of a Type One, so use him to help you judge Ones in real life or in fiction. He is an archetype.
- A difference between a healthy One and unhealthy One (see The Baroness entry) is that unhealthy Ones are smothered by their conflicting emotions and act out sexually or dangerously. Healthy Ones can move beyond their ego identity (and willingly sacrifice themselves), while average or unhealthy Ones still cling to their egos and feel threatened.
- Ones will continually try to reform, improve, and learn.
- A healthy One is near-impossible to defeat in fiction, and usually commit martyrdom rather than being outsmarted.

Other Healthy 1's
Wonder Woman
Wonder Woman, a.k.a. Diana, [DC Comics] is known for being principled, intense, professional, and a soldier. She doesn't give into passion, and is still a virgin. She's too perfect for Superman: she is a truth-seeker and delivers justice with force. Her superpowers are on par with the Man of Steel, and she has additional weapons in her arsenal, such as the lasso of truth and bullet-deflecting bracelets. Wonder Woman is an icon of feminism and independence. Her DC New 52 version acts like a Type 8, however.

Trinity
Trinity [Matrix] is a professional, efficient, and cold hacker-turned-liberator who believes in justice and "the truth." She is the First Officer aboard the Nebuchadnezzar, a common function for Type Ones in science fiction. Trinity acted as a go-between field agent for Morpheus when reaching out to individuals deemed ready to learn the truth about the Matrix. She gave her heart to only one man- Neo, although she initially kept her emotions and the Oracle's prophecy to herself. She revealed the truth when Neo needed to be saved, and remained loyal to him and his cause until the end. Trinity was able to come up with solutions on the fly, literally, and was skilled in hand-to-hand combatant. She acts quickly under pressure. Compare her physical looks to Ursa.

Part Two
Type 2

Beast Man

Fear/Desires: His whole life centers around Skeletor's desires and approval.

Motivations: To rule over others, but he winds up being a slave.

Important Life Events: Found by Skeletor, and dedicating his life to serving him.

Reactions Under Stress: Abuses others, combative, submissive.

Mental Health Range: 7-9

The Wing Slider: 1w2

Instinctive Subtype: Social

Quirks: Complains, being labeled as a servant.

Also Could Be: In his early conceptions, Beast Man is probably an 8 at his core being, but is usually characterized as a sniveling Two.

Beast Man is a villain in the Masters of the Universe franchise, which started off as a toyline in the 1980s and branched into cartoons, comics, and a movie. He is a disgruntled lackey henchman servant and slave of his powerful boss, Skeletor, who is an Enneagram Type 8. Beast Man's entire life is based on his relationship with Skeletor. It's a very typical and pathetic relationship between an Enneagram Type 2 and and Enneagram Type 8, from the unhealthy perspective, of course.

Beast Man's origin varies from cartoons, comic books, toys, and books, but the core character is being a henchman. He's either loyal or forced to be subservient to Skeletor. Like all unhealthy 2's, when his loyalty, actions, love, or recognition is not returned, they feel spurned. They get angry, start plotting, feel victimized, and are symbols of the "spurned lover" archetype. The Beast Man is a great example of that.

The irony is that, although many times, the Two feels victimized in his or her mind, without any proof (for example, it's so easy to slight someone, even if it wasn't an intentional slight), Beast Man is actually physically and mentally abused by Skeletor, especially in the mini-comics that came with the action figures and the Filmation cartoon. So it is justified.

Here's Beast Man: he's Skeletor's loyal, right-hand man, yet Skeletor proceeds to belittle him, shoot bolts from his hand at him, and uses his havoc staff to beat him like an animal He treats him like a dog and totally mocks him. He just abuses him in every way you can think of for no reason at all, other to show his power.

It's so easy to sympathize with Beast Man. In fact, if you were a fan of Masters of the Universe and someone says, "Okay, who was your favorite villain," or, "Which villain did you want to hear more about or sympathize or care about?" People will say, "Oh! Skeletor! Skeletor!"

But when you really start asking, deep down, they're like, "You know, I wish Beast Man would have just hit him, you know?"

In the Masters of the Universe episode "Prince Adam No More" Beast Man gets kicked out of Skeletor's little gang. He really gets humiliated. To show his worth to Skeletor, Beast Man goes back to the wild and recruits Shadow Beasts (who were laughing at his anguish). He hatched a successful scheme to capture King Randor of Eternia, who happens to be He-Man's dad. Although He-Man foils the plot, like he always does, at the end of the episode, Skeletor allows Beast Man to come back in the group.

Sure enough, Skeletor continues to abuse him, and Beast Man apparently loves it. The Enneagram can explain it: it's because 2's want to feel wanted. They like to serve in a role that makes them feel needed.

This is unfortunately shown in abusive relationships, such as the the battered wife syndrome, or an abused husband situation. Usually, the reaction to a victim is, "Why does she going back to him?" Well, a keyword for Enneagram Type Twos is dependency. With dependency comes a love/hate relationship and the feeling of helplessness.

However, modern day interpretations and reboots of the Masters of the Universe have attempted to update Beast Man, by taking him back to his original toy-line roots. Examples include his toy redesign by Mike Young Productions, his revised origin in MVCreations Icons of Evil 1, and his 2008 MOTU Classics toy biography. These changes try to take him back to being a tough monster who is Lord of the Jungle, primal, has dominion over animals, and is a Master of the Universe.

Yet these modern day interpretations can never erase the Filmation treatment of Beast Man as the victimized 2 simply because:

1. Millions of children worldwide watched He-Man cartoons in the 1980's and those kids are now in their 30's and may still collect toys, and

2. when Filmation released the series on DVD, they sold millions of copies, and younger fans also experienced the victimized version of Beast Man.

With many Type 2's, it's so easy to underestimate them. For example, Beast Man sometimes can't control animals. He has problems with dragons. He can't even control Cringer (Battle-Cat, in his civilian identity). That's because of a lack of confidence and concentration. They get nervous. Self-esteem is low and they mentally put these blocks in their mind. The emotions take over, quite possibly the only true weakness of a Two, and the unhealthy Twos completely live in a reality based on their personalized hurt feelings.

Yet, although Beast Man is easy to underestimate, he could be crafty. At times, he does show he could do a good job- he has been shown to control creatures and is a monster with immense strength. If things were different, he could be the King of the Jungle. Maybe he could be the leader of the Army of Beast-Men, which has been shown in some comics, and rule Eternia, or at least overthrow Skeletor.

Unfortunately, he's just so mentally scarred and dependent on Skeletor that, like many other 2's, his mind is gone. Once the psychological damage is done, unhealthy Twos need intensive support and therapy to get back on track. Until then, they could never be a leader of men or women. It's a shame.

A parody gay video featuring Skeletor and Beast Man was released on the internet in the early 2000s. It was a joke video all about their frustrations, yet it really opened up my eyes to the sexual tension that may have existed between those two.

Part of being an unhealthy Two is engaging in submissive, subservient, and subhuman roles, but with the desire to turn the tables, manipulate, and exert control. If not sexual, then the tendency is to play mind games.

Finally, let's compare Twos and Sixes because they both seem "helpful" and "nice". When Enneagram Type 6's exhibit the passive-aggressive tendency and act like martyrs, they can be confused with Twos. Well, the difference is that 6's unconsciously test loyalty and patience of authority figures. The authority figure can be anyone or anything- it could be a symbol. If you happen to be viewed as part of a symbol, like a government agent or post office worker, a disgruntled 6 may start yelling at you. You'll have no idea why he or she is yelling at you. It's not based on intimate or personal relationships, like the 2 does.

The 2 will act up when they feel ignored or unloved by someone who they had invested a lot within a relationship. So, they want something back. The 6 will unconsciously see if the authority figure is legitimate. Can it support them and give them security? Meanwhile, the 2 is just about the relationship with someone they know already. If the Two does yell at a postal worker, it's because the worker was rude or ignored the Two, not because the worker is a symbol of "the system".

We believe most 2's base their relationship expectations on their relationship with their dads. So, they could really set themselves up for pain when they do that in relationships. More than any other type, the Two's whole world revolves around their feelings.

What we've learned:
- Even a minor character in pop culture like Beast Man can reveal an inner truth about the Enneagram, which in turn can help us deal with people (and ourselves).
- Unhealthy Twos are completely skewed due to believing their feelings are reality and permanent.
- Unhealthy Twos are submissive yet also manipulative.
- Eights and Twos make natural couples: The Boss and The Helper, the dominant and aggressive Eight, and the submissive and passive Two.
- Twos feel like victims and will eventually lash out.

- Twos and Sixes have reputations for being nice and agreeable.
- Sixes view people as authority figures, allies, or foes, and lash out at perceived threats.
- Being at an unhealthy level is your personal dark side.
- Twos spend a lot of energy and time on relationships.

Other Unhealthy 2's
Psycho Pirate
The Psycho Pirate [DC Comics] is a mentally unstable villain who has the power to manipulate emotions. The irony is this is what every Type Two can do WITHOUT a Medusa Mask! Showing all the negative traits of an unhealthy Two, the Psycho Pirate is weak, spineless, and exists only to feed off emotions. He became the Anti-Monitor's lackey, another villainous Type 8, during the 1985 Crisis on Infinite Earths maxi-series. He enjoys laughing maniacally and talking to himself about the Multiverse that no one remembers while he is locked up in Arkham Asylum.

The Toad
The Toad [Marvel Comics] is a sniveling villain who has a love/hate relationship with his boss, Magneto (yet another villainous Type 8). After being abandoned by his parents, he was recruited into the Brotherhood of Evil Mutants. The Toad wants Magneto's attention, praise, and approval, but always gets abused by him instead. Years later, during Earth-X, The Toad got revenge by making Magneto his puppet slave. He has a fixation with the Scarlet Witch; fixations on individuals who feed their insecurities is typical for unhealthy Twos. The Ray Park Toad from the X-Men movie seems cooler, which may indicate a shift in personality type.

Marie Barone

The overbearing matriarch of the Barone family, Marie constantly puts herself in the middle of disagreements between her son Ray and his wife Debra. Ray is her favorite, and she makes no attempt to hide this from her older son, Robert. Constantly puts down Debra's cooking and housekeeping skills. Uses her cooking skills to impress her sons and maintain her influence on them. Constantly barks at her husband, Frank, but is also slavishly loyal to his demands, tolerating his abrasive personality.

Edith Bunker

Fear/Desires: Her whole life centered around her daughter and husband, and she lived through them.

Motivations: To have a stable household.

Important Life Events: Getting married, giving birth.

Reactions Under Stress: Panics, cries.

Mental Health Range: 2-5

The Wing Slider: Straight 2

Instinctive Subtype: Social

Quirks: Smothers her daughter, clueless, funny.

Also Could Be: Her parody character, Marge Simpson, is a Nine. Both female Twos and Nines are "homemakers".

All in the Family was one of the most, if not the most, popular American television shows from the 1970s. It had an excellent syndication run, even until today on cable. Although a younger generation may not know about that show, most North Americans over the age of 35 do.

It was a very trendsetting show that tackled racism, homosexuality, women's liberation, rape, miscarriage, abortion, breast cancer, the Vietnam war- adult topics. It got away with a lot of topics on television that, ironically, some shows can't get away with today due to some politically correct groups that would protest them off the air.

Anyway, although Archie Bunker was the star, Edith Bunker was the heart and soul of the show. As an Enneagram Type 2, she was the homemaker, the loving wife and loving mother.

Her head is in the clouds at times and she just wants harmony in the household. She is very submissive to Archie and has a very typical expectation: to be a wife that has to have dinner on the table, as well as respect that her husband has a particular chair in the living room.

At times, she's very slow and not that intelligent. Archie calls her "dingbat" in most episodes, but don't underestimate her. Like some 2's who may not have an aptitude in advanced technology, Edith Bunker has other skills: compassion and a different perspective. She usually has an alternative view on issues that Archie, Mike, and Gloria do not have. Sometimes she has this child-like observation that makes the audience say, "Hmm. Aha. It's so simple, that it's true." And that's what Edith Bunker brings to the table in this show. She has these simple viewpoints that have bigger meanings. This can be observed in almost every episode where they are eating at the table. At times, Edith's joke shows how absurd the debate is.

Although she's a dingbat who often has humorous blunders and stupidity, she really has this unparalleled optimism that the other characters do not have. Optimism and positivism is a natural trait of Twos. After all, if a Two's emotions are her reality, why would she choose to be negative? This is the difference between unhealthy Twos and average Twos. An average Two will smile and have fun, while the unhealthy Two will be consumed by sadness or rage.

So, like many 2's, Edith has an understated wisdom, as well as a wise perception of how life and reality works, more so than the other characters, who are fixated and single-minded. For example, Archie's a racist and a die-hard conservative- demonstrated in every episode. Mike is a bleeding-heart liberal, and has never changed. Gloria is an unrelenting feminist. Well, Edith plays well against all of them, and can see their point of view at times, but always brings a dose of wisdom to it, to have them pause and at least reflect on their extreme viewpoint. Edith is not a racist in any way even though her husband is. She was very welcoming to the Jeffersons, their neighbors in the episode "Lionel Moves Into the Neighborhood".

We personally know and have interviewed a few Twos that pretty much are clones of Edith Bunker. They don't realize it (since self-awareness is not an average Two trait), but they have Edith's warm charm. These Twos bring comedy to the table, are light-hearted, want to have fun, and can always see a good point of view in a negative situation, thanks to their simplicity and humor (intentional or unintentional).

Edith's the perfect tag-team partner and the perfect role player, even though she has her obvious deficiencies (gullible, needs instruction, dependent, has incorrect information). Without a Two in the mix, the show just falls apart, and that happened when the actress Jean Stapleton started to request to be phased out of the show. The quality of the show decreased, and ratings dropped. When she finally left the show, she asked to be killed off. The show focused on Archie grieving and things were just not the same. She was the matriarch of the family.

Now, don't let the fact that Edith is submissive and subservient to Archie make you think that she doesn't speak up. She can be pushed. She is pushed out of fear, especially when Archie is pig-headed about gambling. Edith saw her parents split up because of gambling, as revealed in "Archie the Gambler". So, in order to preserve the family, Edith would speak up, but not in every episode. In fact, in most of the episodes, she doesn't, but there are some memorable times where she actually does raise her voice and put her foot down ("Edith's Problem", "California, Here We Are", "Cousin Liz", and others). The audience gives her a rousing ovation in those moments because it's so epic.

Edith is very protective of her daughter, Gloria, and can be smothering at times. The writers of the show were very clever by making it feel natural, flowing, and ordinary for Edith to be so obsessively concerned about her meek child (who is a Type 9). Edith can show a different side (anger, aggressiveness, and disobedience) when protecting Gloria.

We rated her average, although the case can be made that she's healthy. Basically, she really doesn't work on growth or any spiritual development. She is what she is. She definitely is not unhealthy at all, and she is a textbook loving Two. That's not to say we diminish her at all, especially since she has unconditional love for everyone in her family, and even for total strangers she meets in the street.

The major reason she is usually average is because she generally will absorb Archie's abuse and not stand up for herself. She lets him get away with berating her. The sad part is that without the laughing audience it could very easily be an average household in real life, where one spouse keeps calling the other dumb. Obviously it makes for good comedy, but it does mirror the Type 8 and Type 2 relationship as discussed in the Beast Man entry in this book. In fact, if one reads the dialogue between Archie and Edith, and compares it with the dialogue between Skeletor and Beast Man, one could see the similarities.

We want to be clear that characters and people can still be good, heroic, and productive even at an average level of development. In fact, most of humanity is average, since it's the default setting when we're born. We learn how to be healthy or unhealthy. Not everyone needs to be enlightened or self-actualized. Looking at the avera high on the level of development scale- the high average and low healthy range- as opposed to the low average and high unhealthy range, when you can clearly see and experience major issues with someone.

It's about how we handle ourselves under stress. Edith seems to hold her anger in because she doesn't want to be labeled as a disloyal wife. Many Twos we have spoken with are afraid to speak up out of fear. Ironically, the unhealthy Two will speak up but it will be in an immature, unprofessional, and belligerent way (like a stressed Eight). The natural development scheme of the Enneagram (Two integrates to a Four) encourages Twos to assert their independence in relationships by being self-reliant, confident, and able to express discomfort without walking on eggshells.

The late Florida psychologist Dr. Fred Hinde said it best: "Your feelings are more important than other people's feelings." This means not to accept being stepped on or victimized. It's okay to say "no". You must accept that you can't please everyone all of the time, and it doesn't make you selfish. After all you own your feelings, not anyone else.

What we've learned:

- Twos are capable of compassion, loyalty, and unconditional love- even at the average levels of development.
- Twos needs to stand up for themselves in a proper way to avoid feeling victimized.
- Twos add warmth and fun to relationships or groups.
- Twos are afraid to be labeled as being "bad" or selfish.
- Twos can be both subservient yet a necessary component to a family, and without Edith, Archie is lost.
- The gap between average and unhealthy or average and healthy is *huge* when it comes to spiritual development, happiness, and distress.
- Types who engage in behavior or attitudes which mimic the natural flow of the Enneagram integration are on the "right path".
- Average and unhealthy Eights are shockingly abusive using any standard.
- The Enneagram is so versatile that it can clearly show the relationship between sets of characters that on paper have nothing to do with each other (Beast Man and Edith Bunker; Skeletor and Archie Bunker). Having esoteric knowledge like this allows you to see the makeup of the world.

Other Average 2's
Lt. Commander Troi

Deanna Troi [Star Trek] is the ship's psychologist. She is a natural empath and in touch with everyone's feelings. Troi has a lot of sway with higher ranking officers, as her input is valued when decisions are made. She has loved William Riker and Worf. Troi can disrupt someone's comfort zone or timeline, like the time she forced Picard to befriend a young teenager raised by Talarians. She is also capable of simple insights that are easily missed, like when she figured out that a race of 2-dimensional beings dragging the Enterprise into a deadly cosmic string were doing so purely out of instinct; this led to the solution that allowed the Enterprise to escape their grasp.

R2D2

R2D2 [Star Wars] coincidentally has the number 2 in his name. This Droid is the ultimate helper and sidekick, helping to save C3PO many times (even when he doesn't realize it). He also has a trait that the we coin as the "Time Displacement Authority"- he makes things happen and alters the timeline by getting involved with people's lives (Luke Skywalker, C3PO, Obi Wan, Leia, Anakin, et al). R2D2 is a brave android who will stand up to anyone in order to help his friends/masters. He is great at keeping secrets and flat-out lying. R2 has a great sense of humor, and derives enjoyment from confusing C3PO.

Sue Storm

Invisible Woman [Marvel Comics]- Sue Storm Richards used to be the prototypical "damsel in distress" and the ideal woman of the 1960s before being revamped into a feminist in the 1970s. She was finally shown as the true heart and soul of The Fantastic Four in modern comic books. Sue is loving, family orientated, motherly, yet also extremely powerful and principled. A strong second-in-command, she pulls Reed out of the lab and helps keep him grounded to reality, as well as watching over her younger brother.

Joyce Summers

Joyce Summers [Buffy the Vampire Slayer] is a Baby Boomer mom who tries to make Buffy listen through guilt. Joyce is divorced and had issues raising Buffy on her own, trying to balance work with parenthood. She is not observant and at times very clueless as to what her daughter's private life is. Joyce was initially very angry at Giles for keeping Buffy's status as the Slayer a secret from her, as well as for training Buffy, but eventually took her daughter's mission in stride, providing support to her, as well as Buffy's friends.

Dr. McCoy

Fear/Desires: To care for others.

Motivations: Uses his medical training and skills to take care of and help out the crew of Enterprise, as well as beings who need help that he comes in contact with.

Important Life Events: Appointed chief medical officer of the USS Enterprise. Received Spock's katra before Spock died, and returned it when Spock was reborn.

Reactions Under Stress: Can lose his temper and become argumentative.

Mental Health Range: Lives in the 2 to 6 range.

The Wing Slider: No wing.

Instinctive Subtype: Social.

Quirks: Distrusts technology, which is common among some Type 2's.

Also Could Be: A brief web search for "leonard mccoy enneagram type" reveal some believe he is a Type 1.

Dr. Leonard "Bones" McCoy is the heart of Star Trek: The Original Series. His main function is offering advice to Captain Kirk and debating Mr. Spock's cold logic with passionate and humanistic arguments. Even though McCoy is generally shown as a Healthy Two, he still slips into the Average levels when under distress (usually when his advice is not headed, when a patient is dying, or when arguing with Spock).

McCoy is a compassionate man, as he cares for his patients. He is a firm believer in non-intrusive medicine, and distrusts technology (this is shown in every episode where he complains about using the teleporter, and his comments about using less intrusive healing techniques from *Star Trek IV: The Voyage Home*). Twos being fearful, inept, or distrustful of technology is a quirk that we have observed (although there are exceptions, naturally). Using the examples provided in this book, both Beast Man and Edith Bunker do not have natural aptitudes toward technology.

Bones values friendship and "doing the right thing" over a strict adherence to Starfleet protocol. All of his passionate arguments and opinions stem from his emotions. In this way, he is very stubborn, self-righteous, and prone to expressing anger and frustration. Whereas Spock is like a computer and Kirk is the action hero, Bones is the moral voice. In many ways, viewers can relate to his character more than Spock or Kirk: he's an everyman surrounded by Spock's offensive (yet technically correct) forms of cold logic, and Kirk is always ready to blow the entire ship up with all of his crew before the enemy can board.

In other words, Bones is the most "human" of the triad. That being said, the writers of Star Trek usually show Spock and Kirk being "correct" by taking the high ground, which is usually an impersonal, sacrificial decision that treats everyone as equal. Yet many Twos practice the "needs of the one outweigh the needs of the many", depending on who the person is.

As a Healthy Two, Dr. McCoy enjoys saving lives, healing people, and influencing his crew mates positively. Actions speak louder than words. He does get out of control with his passionate beliefs, and his bigotry against Vulcans for not expressing their emotions, but ultimately he has shown time and time again that he does love Spock as a brother.

So even at healthy levels, Twos (and all other types) retain their egos. It is important to remember that the Enneagram can be used as a blueprint to handle stress, get along with others, and love oneself, but the "goal" is not to become someone boring or pleasure denying. For the Two, being at the healthy levels means lighting up a room with a friendly presence and helping others unconditionally and without judgements. Keep in mind, even though McCoy displays bigotry toward Vulcans, he has never even considered refusing to administer medical treatment. It's just not in his character to be so petty.

McCoy doesn't want others to experience pain, and he is sensitive about the feelings of others and his own pain. *Star Trek V: The Final Frontier* reveals by flashback that McCoy allowed his father to commit suicide to relieve pain. Shortly after doing so, a cure was found, and McCoy carried the guilt with him. Twos and the feeling of guilt go hand-and-hand. They can be consumed by it or they can make others feel guilty. They are truly intimate with that feeling, whether they realize it or not.

McCoy's character has been an inspiration to a generation of fans. The actor, DeForest Kelley, commented that fans would approach him at conventions and tell him they joined the medical professional because of him.

Healthy Twos go above and beyond any expectations that one may have for people. They can give you a break, help you without asking anything in return, have a warm open heart, will not judge you, and share the rarest of all emotions: compassion.

What we've learned:
- Healthy Twos can back up their words and help people by saving lives or offering valuable advice.
- Using the three main Two examples in this book (healthy, average, and unhealthy), you can see how part of a Two's journey is to get over feeling like a victim and to express oneself, which will lead to helping others with no questions asked.
- Healthy Twos can inspire others because they don't ask for anything in return.
- When Twos offer advice, it comes from the human condition and social aspects that tend to be disregarded or forgotten in business, government, military, and other environments.
- Twos enjoy giving advice and teaming up with others, and are invaluable members of a unit.

Other Healthy 2's
Supergirl (DC Comics, Bronze and Silver Age)
Supergirl [DC Comics] (Silver and Bronze Age), more than any other comic book character, showed unconditional compassion, understanding, and forgiveness. She even tried to rehabilitate Lex Luthor. Unlike Sue Richards of the Fantastic Four, Supergirl had no family to take care of (besides her famous cousin, whom she was subservient to), thus she performed noble and helpful deeds under no obligation. She was a saint, which is why it was so sad when she was murdered by the Anti-Monitor in CRISIS.

Part Three
Type 3

Doctor Doom

Fear/Desires: Doom wants to rule the world in his image, and fears Mr. Fantastic's intelligence...although he would never admit it.

Motivations: He had a few: to save his mother's soul, take over the world, and prove his genius is greater than Mr. Fantastic's. He has achieved them all, so he focuses on long-term planning now.

Important Life Events: Death of parents, meeting Reed Richards at college, facial scars, putting the armor on, too many too list after that.

Reactions Under Stress: Plotting. Homicidal. Vindictive. Vengeful.

Mental Health Range: Lives in the 5 to 9 range. Occasionally has been shown to have human insight and in touch with his feelings, but this is usually washed away by the next storyline.

The Wing Slider: Slight 4-wing.

Instinctive Subtype: Self-preservation.

Quirks: Like most Type 3's, is consumed with his image. dictator, melodramatic.

Also Could Be: There does not seem to be any argument online about Dr. Doom's personality type. For argument's sake, you could confuse him with other aggressive types, like 8 or 7.

Marvel Comics' Dr. Doom celebrates his 50th anniversary this year, 2012. In our opinion, he is the greatest of all comic book villains, although IGN disagrees with me when it published its Top 100 Villains (behind The Joker and Magneto). They voted him third, which is ironic, since he is the epitome of an unhealthy Enneagram Type *Three*. To further push the number 3 into the mix, Dr. Doom had three goals that he set himself to achieve. Number one was to save the soul of his mother. Number two was to outdo Reed Richards in every way. Number three was to take over the world.

Well, he accomplished all those three things, over the years. Victor Von Doom freed the soul of his mother Cynthia in the Marvel graphic novel *Dr. Strange and Dr. Doom: Triumph and Torment*. Doom had spent years to free his dead mother's spirit from the clutches of Mephisto (the Devil). Doom even teamed up with the hero Dr. Strange. Doom had learned the mystical arts, something that his nemesis Reed Richards shuns.

And that brings us to 2: Doom outdoing Reed Richards. Throughout the years, it seems that Doom has better social skills, organization, and inventions. Although Doom is consumed by an unhealthy hatred and murderous rage to better Richards, Doom is still a respected (or feared) monarch of Latveria, and is beloved (or feared) by his people. Doom's inventions are more practical than Reed's theoretical constructs, which are used for exploring and investigating. A partial listing of Doom's inventions include perfect humanoid androids, advanced robots, a time machine, mind control devices, mood changing devices, energy stealing machines, nuclear weapons, super-powered armor, computers, force shields, has cured Ben Grimm on numerous occasions, teleporters, cured vampirism, a Heaven breacher, dimensional transporter, and many others.

Perhaps even more telling is that Doom's willpower is superior to Richards'. Reed has been known to lose confidence with his leadership abilities, can't function without the support of his wife Sue, is easily distracted by his experiments, and can make some offensive decisions (taking the wrong side in Marvel's Civil War, forming the Illuminati, and hiding information from his wife as seen in Jonathan Hickman's *Fantastic Four* run).

Meanwhile, Doom defeats the all-powerful Beyonder in Secret Wars 10 on his willpower alone, is immune to the Purple Man's mind-controlling power as seen in *Emperor Doom*, is able to maintain his sanity after being hit with the Dazzler's peak light intensity in issue 4 of her comic book, is able to resist the High Evolutionary's mutation device in *Spiderman and the Fantastic Four* 3, and he shows no fear when in Hell (*Fantastic Four* 507).

We would say Doom is superior to Reed. Doom has also helped his former friend Reed and the Fantastic Four to achieve a greater good (*Heroes Reunited* story arc). Granted, Reed Richards may calculate decimal points a little better than Doom, but if Doom heard that, he would kill us in less than a second.

As far as 3 is concerned, Dr. Doom had conquered the globe in *Marvel Graphic Novel: Emperor Doom*, but grew bored of the bureaucracy. He has been shown to rule alternate earths.

Doom is the epitome of the achiever, the motivator. It's like reading straight out of the Enneagram textbook with Von Doom, which is amazing since he was created decades before any Enneagram book was published, and his creators Stan Lee and Jack Kirby never referenced the Enneagram.

He is charming, attractive, a workaholic, ruthlessly ambitious, impeccably competent, and image-conscious. He is a master politician and schemer, and he overthrew the country of Wakanda in *Doomwar* from within. Of course, if he doesn't get his way, he will resort to murder. Actually, since he practices the ends justify the means, murder and mass destruction are par for the cause in his great scheme.

Doctor Doom is imitated all the time in TV, movies, books, and comics, and other melodramatic forms of entertainment. His most famous imitation is Darth Vader, who is not even a type 3, mind you, but a type 9. Yes, some writers get the Enneagram Types incorrect because they are not aware of them, but when it comes to a masked villain who wants to take over the world via technology or magic, one must look to Doom's influence. Even Magneto- who was created by the same two men- starts off as a Doom clone in his early *X-Men* appearances.

Doom's a tyrant, and most of his people live in fear of him, although, like in many dictatorships, it's the only life they know. Now, it's true, he does give them health care and there's no crime, but that's because he rules with an iron fist. Literally. The rest of the world has to acknowledge and respect Doom as a world leader, because he knows how to play the political game, just like other type 3's.

Being an unhealthy 3, Doom is consumed with his image and he's definitely narcissistic. His original artist jack Kirby stated that Doom's small scar is the incident that had pushed him over the edge. Doom will become vindictive and vengeful, and will ruin other people's happiness. He becomes obsessive and will destroy anyone that points out any of his shortcomings, failures, or arrogance. Yes, he has committed murder. He rationalizes his destructive behavior because he believes in the philosophy of, "by any means necessary," like other warped 3's.

Everything he does is to foster and nurture his image of superiority. Therefore, he can become jealous and have these inflated notions of himself. Granted, Doom is superior in so many ways, that it is hard to argue with his success. Even with all of the evil acts, Doom forces readers to debate his morality,

In fact, in alternate timelines and future timelines, Doom actually cures the entire world of all its ills. If he set his mind to perform good acts, the world would be a much better place. If he can get over his hang-ups with Reed Richards (jealousy), the world would be like a heaven. The technology and magic, and his leadership style, would have assured that humanity would live on in space, and become virtually immortal. All the diseases would have been squashed. Examples of realities such as this include the comic *What If? Secret Wars* and Adam Warlock's Counter Earth.

Instead, Doom likes to focus on little things that damage his ego. Granted, he has a major plan, and the comics have hinted that the reality we just described is his master plan. They do hint that is his true motivation. It does make sense, when you consider he already achieved the three goals he originally set out for.

So, we believe Doom is just biding his time and playing the game until the time is right and his forces are ready, where he will better humanity by any means necessary, in the Machiavellian sense.

Doom has defeated anyone that crossed his path. Although his win/loss record is bad, it could easily be written off as him pretending to lose, or him having a robot double that takes the fall. You have to understand, Doom always has a greater plan. Anytime he loses, it's just a minor setback or all part of the master plan.

Another great accomplishment of Doom is that his master, the Marquis of Death, actually had sent him back 50 million years into the past, yet Doom survived, persevered, all on the sheer power of his will and hate, as well as his love for himself, and the fact that he can never be beaten in the end. He actually just waited him out, and sure enough, it became the present time, and Doom defeated the Marquis of Death. This storyline occurs in *Fantastic Four* 566-569.

If he put his mind to it, he could just destroy anything or anyone.

The subject of nature versus nurture is very important with Doom. The tragedy of his parents dying really made him flip out. His mother was a gypsy witch. His father was a rebel. Doom couldn't handle the deaths of his parents. He had to prove something to the world: that he was competent. Threes must prove something. They must create an image to prove their value, that they're worthy. The image becomes so real that they lose touch with their humanity.

Originally, Doom came off as a crazy perfectionist, as well. He felt devalued with that scar. In the 1980s we were shown via flashbacks that he had put on a hot-iron mask to totally create this Doom persona, as well. First, it was a little scar, then he was totally disfigured, so he could fit into that role because, to him, his face was imperfect anyway. Please note that there are other takes of Doom from various creative teams, but we are focusing on the most famous versions.

In the end, Doom is the ultimate unhealthy Three. He is just so efficient, superior, and pragmatic, and such a natural leader, with intelligence and powers that all come from hard work. Yet he chose the evil path. Doom is a great villain because there is just so much there to work with. So much more than the Joker, who is just insane. Not that there's anything wrong with the Joker as a character, but you can't even compare the two.

What we've learned:
- Unhealthy Threes are dangerous because they won't hesitate to attack others, while other unhealthy types are prone to be self-destructive,
- Threes are natural performers and can create fantastic roles and images.
- Threes have a natural aptitude to succeed in life. Although intelligence is not a personality trait, being adaptable and social is. Threes have a tendency to rise to the top in politics, sports, business, and other social networks.
- Threes know "how the world works" and are extremely pragmatic. They generally shun theoretical philosophies.
- Threes love action, being productive, and learning new skills.
- Unhealthy Threes are too egocentric, conceited, and will believe their own hype. Therefore, they are prone to taking extreme risks. This may be okay in fiction (Dr. Doom can never die because his stories and will exist), but not in real life, where Threes may overextend themselves.
- Threes are self-motivated, self-made, and are prime candidates for "rags to riches" stories.
- Unfortunately, unhealthy Threes are prone to lying, cheating, stealing, and killing in order to cling to their image and to achieve their goals.

Other Unhealthy 3's
Maxwell Lord
Maxwell Lord [DC Comics] is a ruthless, clever, power hungry, and manipulative businessman. He manipulates major events behind the scenes, including the formation of the Justice League of America, which he financed- a conspiracy theorist's dream. He simply cannot be trusted and is a known liar. Maxwell Lord is highly intelligent in politics, business, technology, and scheming. He hides behind the respectability of money and suits.

The Master
The Master [Buffy the Vampire Slayer] was an ancient vampire committed to scheming to bring about the destruction of earth and to assure his immortality. The Master was extremely melodramatic, and seemed to be tapping into the common phrases from the Three Dimension. The Master wanted to be worshiped, and was extremely arrogant and selfish.

Emperor Palpatine
A grand manipulator, the man who would become Emperor Palpatine [Star Wars] is introduced to us in Episode I as a senator from the planet Naboo during the reign of Queen Amidala. He became Supreme Chancellor by playing both sides of a dispute to his advantage, using his Darth Sidious identity to influence the Trade Federation into starting a

blockade. Increasingly, the true nature of Palpatine begins to surface, until he is disfigured during a climactic battle with Mace Windu. Eventually, decades after declaring himself Emperor of the "First Galactic Empire", his hubris finally caught up with him, as he took for granted that Darth Vader would do nothing and remain loyal, even as he attempted to murder Vader's son, Luke Skywalker.

Regina Mills

The Evil Queen from Fairytale Land, Regina Mills [Once Upon a Time], cursed everyone to live in our modern reality, all to prevent her perceived enemy Snow White from experiencing a happily ever after. Regina, in season one of the show, is Mayor of Storybrook, and one of the few characters to retain memories of Fairytale Land. She will do anything to keep her adopted son Henry away from his birth-mother Emma. She is always acting from a skewed notion of reality. She is vain and determined to hold on to her power. She appears to be another example of an unhealthy Type 3 who uses magic and the dark arts to her advantage. Since it is season one of the show as of this writing, there is still lots to be revealed about her. It is possible that she might turn out to have another personality type.

Khan

Khan Noonien Singh is a Sikh modeled after conquerors and leaders of old, such as Napoleon and Richard the Lionhearted, in the 1960's Star Trek episode, "Space Seed." He demonstrates his intelligence and tactical skills by learning 200 years worth of engineering and technical material and briefly taking over the Enterprise, with a contingency planned for every move Kirk and Spock could come up with. His weakness is his romantic side, which leads to his defeat in the episode. This weakness becomes his driving motivation during Star Trek II: The Wrath of Khan, when he seeks to kill now-Admiral Kirk for forgetting him on Ceti Alpha 5, a planet that was knocked out of orbit 6 months after being dropped off there with his wife and crew. The planet went from a lush place full of possibilities to a desert planet, and Khan, through sheer force of will, managed to survive for 15 years while waiting for his chance to strike. In Star Trek: Into Darkness, we're introduced to an alternate version of Khan. Like the original, this Khan is deceitful and manipulative, and exhibits superhuman physical abilities.

Tony Stark

Fear/Desires: To create a better world.

Motivations: Uses technology and politics to make the world a safer place.

Important Life Events: Built the Iron Man suit. A leading force behind the Superhero Registration Act.

Reactions Under Stress: Can become incredibly manipulative and lose touch with his feelings.

Mental Health Range: The Iron Man from the movies and Civil War comic mini-series is in the average range of 4 - 6.

The Wing Slider: Does not appear to have a wing type.

Instinctive Subtype: Social.

Quirks: Took Peter Parker under his wing during Civil War, which was similar to how the Emperor from Star Wars, another Type 3, became a mentor to Anakin Skywalker.

Also Could Be: Before the movies and Civil War, Tony Stark was a Type 7 who struggled with alcoholism and was a bit rebellious. While Robert Downey Jr. occasionally taps into this edgy side, the more recent incarnation of Iron Man, in our estimation, is a Type 3.

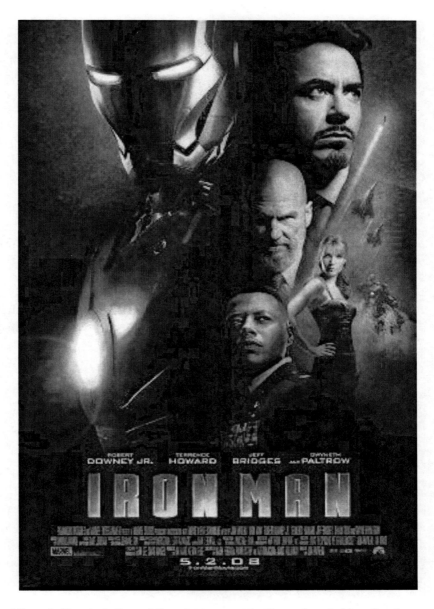

Marvel Comics' Iron Man has catapulted to the A-List thanks to Robert Downey, Jr.'s portrayal of Tony Stark/Iron Man on the silver screen starting in 2008. However, comic book fans have liked Iron Man for decades. For the majority of Iron Man's publishing history, he's a Type 7. However, writer JMS (J. Michael Straczynski) put his Enneagram Type 3 touch into the character during Civil War, a 2006 major event in Marvel history. Parts of that character were put into the *Iron Man* movies and *Avengers*.

That's not to say that Iron Man acts like a 3 in every scene in *Iron Man 1, 2,* and *Avengers* because Robert Downey Jr. seems to tap into the 7 character much better than 3. However there are aspects of it to kind of confuse the situation. For the purposes of this section, we're going to be focusing on Iron Man as a 3.

During the Civil War, it was revealed that Iron Man was part of the Illuminati that teamed up with the other major powers at the beginning of the Marvel Universe- behind the scenes- to plot, keep the status quo, and to act when the status quo gets out of control, or when they need to intervene. These big-wigs include such players as Professor X, Reed Richards, Doctor Strange, Black Bolt, and Namor the Sub-Mariner. These were big power players, and Iron Man was the force behind it. Writer Brian Michael Bendis wrote their origin in *New Avengers: Illuminati* 1.

Behind-the-scenes manipulation. Conspiracy. Believing the ends justify the means. Practicing "By any means necessary." These are traits out of the Type 3 textbook. That's not to say that 7's don't plot, or any other type doesn't plot. Being an Enneagram type doesn't mean you have an exclusive ownership over an emotion or activity.

For example, anyone can be loyal, not just Loyalists (Type 6). Anger is an emotion felt by every type, even if some don't express it quickly. It's close-minded to say, "Oh, well that guy expressed his anger. He must be a Type 8." It doesn't work that way. We hope that by reading through this book you can see the trends to develop your instincts to make proper judgements.

Tony Stark, in addition to all this manipulation, also completely crossed the line by taking a gullible and naive Peter Parker under his wing, acting as a skewed mentor to him (*Amazing Spider-Man* 535+) . It almost parallels the Emperor from *Star Wars* (also a Type 3) manipulating Anakin Skywalker (Type 9).

A Type 3 once gave one of the authors advice in a certain way like that, and his warning buzzers just went off. The Three said, "Damian, I can teach you how to tap your mind so you can appear in multiple places at once on the Earth and to see that your ego is just an illusion. You can be one with God, and we're all God."

While all that is fine and dandy, and it may technically be true that we're all God, depending on what philosophy you believe in. Or perhaps the self is an illusion, which is true. That's what personality and the Enneagram is. It's simply a mask that we choose to wear. That we must wear. That we must integrate out of and roll with to better ourselves.

However, this Three tried to teach Damian out of selfish reasons. He wanted to manipulate him to become his ally to further his own power base and political career, so to speak, in the office life. He had followers, and when we say followers, we truly mean sycophants: people that would defend him, cover things up, and do things without the real boss knowing.

That's what Iron Man did with Peter Parker/Spider-Man. He was a great motivator for Peter. He was a great inspiration. You can see that in the *Iron Man* movies, as well: how inspiring Tony Stark can be. But there's the root in selfishness and feeding his ego. Stark also keeps secrets from Parker (such as the minor detail that the villains are held in a Guantanamo Bay metaphoric prison, and that Captain America would have to be hunted down.) Iron Man had an agenda similar to the situation in the 1985 limited series Squadron Supreme, where a hero, instead of defending against crime or corruption or whatever you want to call it, actually takes the initiative to prevent it from ever happening in the first place.

So, Iron Man forces the Superhero Registration Act upon everyone, where every hero must reveal his or her identity or be locked down in a prison he created in the negative zone with Reed Richards. This mirrored what was happening with the US government at the time ("You're either with us or against us.") The United States of America right now is the embodiment of an Enneagram Type 3.

There were actually people that had nothing to do with terrorism, 9-11, or Al-Qaeda that ended up in Gitmo, and they are actually still there. No one wants to release them. They can't be released. What was happening in Marvel Comics at that time was a direct analogy to that situation. Iron Man was the center of it.

So, here we have this great, classic hero acting in a way that rubbed people wrong, although he always had an edge. There were other storylines where Iron Man acted out of bounds and came head-to-head with Captain America, such as Armor Wars and Operation Galactic Storm. Type 7's don't like to follow orders. So, he always had that edge where he wasn't a true company man, but JMS really pushed him to be the ultimate company man, the ultimate 3, standing behind that American flag, taking your civil rights away in the name of security.

Additionally, Iron Man is so pig-headed about the way he rationalized his views to impose this law on everyone. It actually resulted the death of Captain America. That's what wakes him up and pulls him back to reality. He is no longer the "Most hated Marvel hero" anymore.

Ultimately, yes: we grade modern Iron Man as an average Type 3. He feels justified in his actions. His actions had good intentions that weren't truly evil because when you have power and you have money, and you can actually make changes to this Earth to make it better.

We've seen the US trying to impose that and, as Ron Paul says, "There's always blowback." Iron Man had the blowback, and he paid for it. He eventually lost his positions, and he had to start over from scratch again.

A problem with fiction in general, in terms of showcasing personalities of characters with longevity, is that a writer can come along and simply change aspects of the personality without truly paying homage or keeping the character in tune with continuity.

For example, Superman started off as an Enneagram Type 8, and then he morphed into a 3. That is not part of the Enneagram matrix. It doesn't work like that. That's based on the fact that writers have different agendas and interpretations of characters. The case could be argued that Peter Parker started off as a Type 4. When Steve Ditko left Amazing Spider-Man, Stan Lee Asserted more authority to convert Peter to a full-fledged 6. With Iron Man, Stan Lee created him off as a playboy and industrious Type Seven in 1963, but JMS/Bendis wrote him as a Three. The movies show him as both.

What we've learned:
- Fiction is not an exact science for interpreting Enneagram personality types for two reasons: 1) Different writers have their own stories and takes on characters and 2) Most writers don't know about the Enneagram, although many times they are able to inadvertently "get it right".
- Threes and Sevens are similar in that they are both action oriented, productive, have manic energy, and are confrontational. Using Tony Stark as an example, one difference is that a Three is more prone to withhold the truth from "followers", manipulate others, play politics, and impose beliefs and morality on others. Sevens can actually function by themselves (or with a sidekick) while Threes feel more comfortable with entourages or troops.
- Threes make natural "bad guys" as easily as they can be natural "good guys". They have extreme and dominant personalities.
- Threes and Sevens don't meet on the Enneagram. A Three integrates into a Six, and disintegrates into a 9.
- We believe places and things also have personalities. In addition to the United States being a Three, the New York Yankees and Miami Heat are two sports teams that are Threes. The Yankees fan base expects to be 1 every season, and not winning the World Series would be a failure. The Yankees are beloved in NY and despised in the other states due to their success and payroll.
- Sixes and Nines can be susceptible to listening to a strong Three when it comes to learning new skills and having a better life. They may ignore the signs that they could be going for a ride.

Other Average 3's
Hyperion

Hyperion [Marvel Comics] is Marvel's skewed version of Superman: he uses his powers to change the world to create a Utopia. He's prone to jealousy, rage, and demands to be recognized for his achievements. He talks down to the sheep. Of course, as Superman already knows, you CAN'T use your powers to change social issues, the economy, or governments. Threes don't understand that people have free will. What do you think Hitler, another Type 3, would have done if he had Superman's power?

Ozymandias

Ozymandias [DC Comics] is a Machiavellian villain who believes in the greater good by any means necessary. The smartest man in the world, he also is an Olympian who built a business and criminal empire (after giving away his inheritance as a teenager). Self-made, his superiority complex and hubris is unmatched in the Watchmen Universe. He is the master schemer at a grand scale, and not a stock villain- he is a skewed hero who believes his moves are righteous and will have positive results.

Namor

Namor [Marvel Comics] demands worship and adoration (he IS the King of Atlantis), has a BAD temper, is vengeful, cannot be controlled, and is powerful. He swings from being a villain and a hero, and from alliance to alliance. He has a different edge than a standard Three like Dr. Doom, due to having a two-wing. His true weakness is his love for Susan Richards, but that centers on his being unable to check his emotions, like other Threes. Both Doom and Namor love Sue and envy Reed. They both would like to see him dead.

He-Man

He-Man [Masters of the Universe] is "the most powerful man in the universe". He's also the most morally superior and best looking. Impossible to defeat, he represents the forces of nice, clean, wholesome, Christian goodness. He-Man loves to lecture and teach. He never compromises his principles and actually teamed up with and forgave Skeletor to combat a common foe. Note: The Iron Cross on his chest, muscles, tan, and blond hair also shows his superiority. A simple version of Superman.

Superman

Fear/Desires: To be the best man and Superman possible.

Motivations: To promote truth, justice, and the American way with his amazing super powers.

Important Life Events: Discovered by Ma and Pa Kent after crash-landing from the doomed planet Krypton. Moving to Metropolis.

Reactions Under Stress: Can be condescending and unfeeling at times.

Mental Health Range: Superman is relatively healthy, with occasional slides into the average range. He lives in the range of 1 through 5.

The Wing Slider: Does not appear to have a wing type.

Instinctive Subtype: Social.

Quirks: Like America and the Yankees, is hated by some for being the best.

Also Could Be: Originally started out as a Type 8, and has recently been returned to this type in the comic books by the writers. Has also shown type 6 tendencies when using his alter-ego, Clark Kent.

Enneagram Pop!   Fictional Characters

Perhaps more than any other character or type, Superman is the living embodiment of his type, which is an Enneagram Type 3. You can't learn or meet Enneagram Type 3's, read about them or actually meet one, without thinking about Superman. It's just one of those things that really shows you the Enneagram is a superior system when compared to any other personality type systems.

The Superman that the Baby Boomers all the way up to the current generation have been raised with is the Superman who is the greatest and first of all heroes. He is 100% heroic, unstoppable, invincible, and always wins. He has super-intelligence, super-strength, super-speed, super-morality, super-breath, and super-looks. It just goes on and on. The man is perfect in every single way. Before Generation X, he was idolized.

So you may consider, "Well, I thought 1's were supposed to be 'perfect'. Aren't they the perfectionist Enneagram Type?" In the Iron Man chapter, we discuss how characters or types don't have an ownership over a particular trait. The perfectionism that 1's strive for is usually a question over right and wrong. The right and wrongness has to do with debates, ethics, or religion. They strive for perfection and doing the right thing.

The Enneagram Type 3 perfection model is to truly build themselves up to be perfect in every way, from the physical standpoint to the mental standpoint, and the spiritual standpoint, with the end-goal that people around them will begin to mimic them, worship them, and buy into their image. Now, Superman is healthy, so he's gotten past that stage. He doesn't need to be idolized. He does it because he has the ability to do it. He does it based on self-actualization.

Superman is 100% genuine. He does things out of the benevolence of his own heart. It doesn't matter what you think of him. He's still going to strive to save you, or the world, or fight evil, or protect you.

For example, let's compare Superman to Mr. Spock from *Star Trek*. They're both healthy and they both seem perfect, but when you compare them, you can see that Superman has many more abilities and skills. So, I believe the perfection factor is that 3's generally strive to be 100% well-rounded. They can do everything and anything. There's not one language they can't learn. They're going to have multiple jobs at once. They're going to be experts in various schools of thought. We've worked with some 3's who just like to rub that in, that they're just not an expert in one topic- but all topics. For example, a 1 may be content with being the best architect, the most perfect writer, the most efficient production manager. That's their niche.

The 3, however, must be the master of all schools of thought and knowledge, or at least attempt to, or at least cover up that he or she is deficient in some areas. Healthy 3's shouldn't care, but they're still going to try to become well-rounded, just to become the best that they can be. A friend of mine is going to medical school and a 60-year-old student applied. I took a look at his resume and it was right out of a Type 3 section, right from the textbook. It listed all of his military credentials, listed his computer-technical credentials, listed his religious chaplain credentials, listed his charities, and now, at 60 years old, after accomplishing all there is to accomplish, he wants to become a doctor.

Most people are thinking retirement at that point. Oh, by the way, he also has real estate deals going on. He lasted one year and then quit due to dissatisfaction with the school organization and professors.

Threes want to do everything and they don't want to rest. We're not disparaging that at all, after all that's what American society expects of its citizens, and to each his own. But Threes can't help it. Compare them to average Type 9's or an unhealthy Type 9. Generally, the typical 9 is going to be a slacker, or if that word is too strong, the 9 has problems with initiative. He or she is going to have to be motivated by others around them. That's where 3's come in. A world without 3's is a world without motivation. They're so industrious, productive and high-spirited that people like to copy them and to mimic them.

This is true in the Superman character. Superman is the most mimicked character in all of comics. It's not just the cape, the boots, the belt, and the symbol on the chest, although that does play a large part in it; it's the fact that the dozens of heroes and villains copy his aura of being unbeatable, the best. In addition, they all have some sort of strict morality like he has.

With Superman being Mr. Perfect, you can understand that some people resent that. Enneagram Type 3's are unconsciously or subconsciously resented by people. For example, the United States of America right now is an Enneagram Type 3. They're the sole remaining superpower, enforce their foreign-policy on the nations, and spread capitalism to third world countries to improve them, so they will become trading partners. All that is well and good, but it still makes some countries upset.

Some people will never admit this, but they don't like someone who is proactive and intervenes in their lives because the impression they get is that they're inferior. Threes, although they can be so inspiring, and such a great benefit to humanity and to individuals when they focus, can make you feel small. They're so larger-than-life they can rub you the wrong way. That's what happens with the United States of America, in terms of their international relations. That's what happens to the New York Yankees. The Yankees are beloved in New York and surrounding areas.

Go to any of the other states and they're going to say, "I hate the Yankees!"

Why do they hate the Yankees? "Well, you know, they have unlimited money. They already won all those championships. They're always in first place. They must be arrogant, right?"

No, they're not arrogant. Derek Jeter is a Type 9, healthy. Mariano Rivera is healthy 4 who integrates into a 1. CC Sabathia is a very generous Type 6. You can go through the list and it's a bunch of nice guys. They have a nice manager, Joe Girardi. The general manager is kind of cocky, but he actually has a lot of fans online. They like his cockiness. So, for people to say they hate the Yankees? That's based on the Yankees being a Type 3- the aura that Threes give. Striving for the best can turn some people off. Ever since they got Babe Ruth in 1919 the Yankees have been the best., and people have to naturally hate number one. Otherwise it's like rooting for Goliath against David.

The same goes for, say, Hulk Hogan in wrestling. Some people have to hate Hulk Hogan because he never lost during his run, from 1984 until 1990, when he fought the Ultimate Warrior and got pinned. We would say Generation X and Y find Superman boring because he's Mr. Unbeatable.

That's why Spider-Man is so popular, because he's so flawed. He's like a born loser, right? People like that human edge. In the 1990s to 2000s writers have tried to give Superman a human edge. How it backfires is if you keep him a 3 but give him a human edge, he acts like a wimp who pulls his punches. It really doesn't work, right? In DC's mega-event *Infinite Crisis*, part of it was about Superman not living up to his image, and he even had to fight his earlier Type 8 version.

Superman started out as a depression era Type 8. He was a product of the times. He was created by two Jewish creative men who were immigrants. The whole attractiveness about Superman was that he lived the American dream, and it wasn't for selfish purposes. He actually defended the rights of minorities, of victims, and of squatters. Let's just say he would be at Occupy Wall Street, if that existed in the 1930's or

40's. He was a worker's rights kind of guy. He hated corrupt landlords. He was not a representative of the US government. In the late 30's and 40's, he was his own man. You couldn't tell him what to do. You can see this by reading any early issue of *Action Comics*.

Over time, after the original creators left, after the war, sometime in the 1950s, the editor at DC decided to make Superman more mainstream. In the 50s, being mainstream was being a square for the white, rich establishment. Thus, Superman would be the mouthpiece of the US president. Truth, justice and the American way became whatever the president wanted without question. It became being respectful of authority, even in the 1960s. This is why DC missed the boat. Again, this is something so widespread in his comics, where you can pick up any *Superman* or *Action Comics* issue from that time period and feel this.

Stan Lee and Marvel we're doing all sorts of experimental stuff in the 60s. They were targeting college students. They were making their characters human and flawed, and to an extent, anti-establishment. Marvel heroes were hunted by the police or had the military shoot at them. Spider-Man, the Hulk, and X-Men were not accepted by society in their stories. They're outcasts. It's totally the opposite of Superman, who was the establishment in the 50s, 60s, 70s, 80s, even in the 1990s and early 2000s, although they tried to soften him up a little bit (got married, had long hair, was depowered, second-guessed himself, needed time-outs).

Grant Morrison has taken over the reins of the creative leadership at DC comics and he put Superman back to being an Enneagram Type 8 in DC New 52. This new Superman is very proactive. He breaks the law. He's not deputized at first. He goes after corrupt corporations, and he evened things up in Libya in a panel in *Justice League*. He wants to cure world hunger.

So, he's back to his roots...depending on the writer. Morrison, along with Geoff Johns, are writing him as an 8, not a 3. Yet, in terms of public consciousness, the general public has not bought the first 10 issues of the new *Action Comics*. They don't know that Superman has that change in personality. They just see that different costume, if they see it at all.

That's the way things are in comics. Most people just remember the movies, cartoons, and TV shows, depending on their age.

Speaking of which, the Superman as portrayed in the movies and TV shows sometimes doesn't seem quite right. Sometimes they show Superman as a 6 or a 9. It makes sense to be on that triad on the Enneagram of 3-6-9. Generally, the movies and TV shows do get that right, in terms of him being on the Triad or showing him as an 8. They never get it wrong by making him a 1, 2, 4, 5, 7. That just shows you how everyone generally knows Superman's personality type.

Look, Wikipedia says he's widely regarded as an American icon. Well, they didn't have to sparse those words. There's no reason to say, "Widely regarded," okay? He is an American icon. He is the ultimate symbol of America. He is the ultimate symbol of Enneagram Type 3's.

Although Superman is healthy in every single way, in the 1960's all the way up until fairly recently, even though he's healthy, he still has that unconscious swagger and is prone to lecturing others. He'll never come out and say he's superior- not even the thought bubbles and the captions. You have to read in-between the panels and the lines. Some writers and artists are better than others at portraying him, but overall, he has that cocky edge. He has that slight haughty nature where he's secretly jealous if someone is trying to get Lois Lane, if someone else gets a headline, or if someone else comes close to him in power levels. He won't come out and say it, but it is part of the 3 nature. If there's competition, they're always going to have to outdo the competition. That's part of the drive that he has. See *All-Star Superman* for a modern take of Superman's swagger.

Superman has also been shown to have some psychological issues. Who is the secret identity? Is it really Clark Kent, or is it Superman? Which is the mask? He jumps from being a 3 to a 6 in the comics. Clark Kent is the 6 in the comics: the nice guy and awkward trooper, generally speaking. He's Mr. Establishment, wearing those glasses, hat, and tie, tripping all over the place, which 6's like to do. That's a joke, by the way. In the New 52, he's not a Six. He's a whiny journalist/blogger who is also very outspoken.

Superman has some psychological issues there, lying to everyone to keep that secret. Why does he need a secret identity anyway? He could be working 24 hours a day to save everyone, as seen in a pastiche hero in *Astro City*. The writers say that he has a secret ID to get in touch with humanity, since he's an alien and was raised by humans. That makes sense, I guess, but it's just a gimmick.

The bottom line is that he lies to keep an image and he's competitive, so he shows you that even though he may be the greatest 3 since ... himself, he still can fall into the trap of making you feel small, like all 3's do, even the healthy ones. And they secretly love it. (Another joke.)

What we've learned:
- Even healthy Threes maintain their image of being the best at something, or completely well-rounded.
- Healthy Threes can change the world positively in major ways.
- Reinforced concepts: a) Threes are envied/despised by some people for being "the best" or 1 at something. b) Places and things can have personalities. c) Different writers and different media may portray a character with a different personality, and it may not make any sense from the Enneagram standpoint.
- Threes don't like giving up and will fight to the end.

Other Healthy 3's
Data
Data [Star Trek] tries to prove his worth by creating an image of being irreplaceable. Indeed, without his technical expertise and strength, the Enterprise would have been destroyed. The android is not human, but has achieved so much in Starfleet that he was granted full civil rights. He eventually experienced emotions. In the end he sacrificed himself, but his personality lives on in another android body; he is virtually immortal, and the most powerful of all crew members. He has superior morals.

Captain America
Captain America [Marvel Comics] is a 3w4. He's a typical Three when in action, but Steve Rogers is a man out of time. When he was younger he was a weakling and was into self-improvement. The bottom line is that Cap is more human than Superman as an American symbol, and in many ways is a greater symbol, since the U.S. started out like a weak outcast full of doubt as Cap did. But, when Cap is "on" he is the ultimate inspirational leader and motivator, better than Uncle Sam.

Ric Hunter
A 19-year-old pilot in Pop Hunter's flying circus, Ric Hunter [Robotech] is thrown into military service when the Zentraedi invade the Earth. He quickly adapts and becomes a squadron leader with the Robotech Defense Force. Ric constantly risks his life to save his friends.

He endures massive tragedy and finds the strength to carry on. Eventually, he chooses Lisa Hayes over Minmay when he realizes he feels true love for her, and that his relationship with Minmay lacks substance.

Part Four
Type 4

Spike

Fear/Desires: To rebel.

Motivations: Expresses his desire through his many loves, as well as his attempts to bring a new age of darkness to humanity.

Important Life Events: Falling in love with Drusilla. Turning over a new leaf and becoming a help/love interest to Buffy.

Reactions Under Stress: Drink blood. Sulk.

Mental Health Range: Shows a lot of range, from the 3 to 9.

The Wing Slider: No wing.

Instinctive Subtype: Sexual.

Quirks: Like some 4's, is anti-everything. Also was known to express himself through poetry prior to becoming a vampire.

Also Could Be: It's possible he's an insane type 2 who degenerates to 8. Possible, but not likely.

Enneagram Type Fours have a lot of personality range, perhaps more than all the other Enneagram types. They can be passionately romantic or disciplined, under-express their emotions, or over-express them with bursts of anger. They can speak through their artwork, writing, or or other creative outlet, or simply not express anything at all. They can embrace individuality and free will, fight society in different ways, or become isolated and live as a hermit.

This may sound contradictory to the notion that no type can own an emotion or trait, but at their core, we could use one word to generalize each type:

One: Reforming
Two: Helping
Three: Achieving
Five: Investigating
Six: Being loyal
Seven: Enthusiastic
Eight: Controlling
Nine: Being peaceful

But Fours? They seem like jacks of all trades. To label them as romantics isn't fair, since many aren't into romance, although finding the ideal mate is a life goal for many Fours (yet some won't admit it, realize it, or act in a way to show this). To call them individualists implies they they all rebel in some way or won't team up. To name a type "The Artist" takes away from all other types. It seems like Fours are naturally creative, but many will say they don't have a creative bone in their bodies. Identifying a Four is hard for many Enneagram novices and experts because they are like chameleons and don't express themselves traditionally. The easy Fours are the ones who latch on to an identity they created, and act threatened when it is questioned. If we had to choose one description to fit a Four, we'd go with "Creative", which does not necessarily imply an aptitude for the arts.

Well, Spike from Buffy the Vampire Slayer is an easy Four, in terms of exhibiting this range. Some Fours we know in real life don't exhibit that full range, or have a strong Three or Five wing, which heavily influences them. We've worked with quite a few computer programmers who are Enneagram Type 4's who, frankly, were exhibiting their creativity through their programs without even realizing it, but they didn't show any other genres a Four can dive in.

Spike had been poet when he was human- and not a very good one- as shown in the flashback episode "Fool's Love" from *Buffy the Vampire Slayer* Season Five. He tended to focus on the melodramatic aspects of romance: longing, desire, and beauty. He also is an exception to the rule of vampires in that he retained his entire personality. Even as a "Soulless" vampire, he exhibited these same things.

Why? He is a strong-willed Four.

In the Buffy-verse, when people get bit by vampires, their souls are gone, and they become some kind of skewed version of themselves, but it seems like when Spike became a vampire around 150+ years ago, it exemplified, enhanced, and kept most of his personality. Of course, he was more free to be cruel, and darker as a vampire, but he's pretty much the same (just prone to killing- out of necessity).

Love and romance follows Spike around his entire life. He loved his mother a little too much. He had been rejected by Cecily, who he had been courting. Then he was bitten by Drusilla, who is a skewed Enneagram Type 5. Although he was dedicated and subservient to her, she had a relationship with Angel, another vampire, and that drove Spike crazy. Spike also had fallen in love with other women throughout his many centuries of existence, including in modern times his arch-rival, Buffy Summers. (The first hint of this occurs in "Out of My Mind", when he has dreams about her.)

Of all the characters in the Buffy-verse, Spike is the one that shows the most growth. He actually starts off as a villain and, in the end, becomes an anti-hero. He becomes a sympathetic figure in Season Three when a microchip is implanted in his brain, which inhibits his aggressiveness. Spike becomes depressed and suicidal, a trait of unhealthy Fours.

It is important to focus on the notion that Spike rebels against the norm and that's what a good chunk of 4's do. There is a class of 4's that will go against conventional wisdom, show innovation, and truly do something revolutionary. There's a class of 4's that are exceptions to every rule, and Spike is one of them.

So Spike has the romantic angle, the exception angle, the creativity angle (with the poetry bit), and the rebel without a cause gimmick. Spike has the British punk rock act going for himself. His style, his dress, and his speech patterns reek of rebellion. He also has an excellent, dry sense of humor, a swagger, and is deadly sarcastic. Amazingly enough, this cold-blooded murderer was comic relief in *Buffy the Vampire Slayer*.

He's very perceptive, self-aware, brutally honest, a critic, and intelligent- all hallmarks of a Type Four. He really gets off on mocking and making fun of his partners or enemies. He appreciates beauty, jokes, and the thrill of hunting and killing.

Ultimately, the main reason why Spike can never become a healthy 4 and integrate into a Type 1- which is a fully disciplined individual who has harnessed, focused, and mastered his emotions- is because of his lust for blood. And some 4's have an urge, or vice, which they cannot overcome. In Spike's case, it is the urge to drink blood. It is the number one desire and passion in his life, which even overtakes his desire to love and appreciate women, nature, and the arts.

Some 4's, especially the troubled ones, are prone to addiction, whether it be alcohol, drugs, sex, or something else. That's why Spike is a fantastic Enneagram Type 4 to feature in this book. The bottom line is that he combines all the different elements that make up a 4. It makes Spike one of the most beloved and memorable characters in the *Buffy the Vampire Slayer* Universe.

What we've learned:
- Fours are the most versatile of all the types and hard for some to label.
- Fours are exceptions to rules.
- Fours under-express their emotions, and may overcompensate with their creativity.
- Unhealthy Fours are prone to depression, becoming addicted to a self-destructive behavior, and suicide.
- Fours are prone to falling in love with the idea of love over the actual lover, getting attached, and display a passive-aggressive nature in a relationship.
- Creativity doesn't necessarily refer to art: it could be writing, music, programming, coming up with new ideas at work or home, thinking outside of the box in conversation, developing a new method of doing something, or other ways.
- Fours will build an image for themselves to aid them in a quest for identity. They will subconsciously or consciously "act the role".
- Fours are self-critics and will not hesitate to criticize others.
- Unhealthy Fours are dangers to themselves and others.

Other Unhealthy 4's
Destro
Destro [G.I. Joe] is part of the terrorist group called COBRA, but he works for himself first. Although he does obey Cobra Commander out of duty, principle, and honor, he has personal projects and arms dealings that he does outside of the organization. He just sees terrorism as a job- he is more concerned with his romance with The Baroness. A great worker, Destro really stands out in COBRA as his own man, yet also retains the image of being a company man.

Rorschach
Rorschach [DC Comics] is an unhealthy Four, from a disintegrated Type One. A depressed, cynical, moody, anti-social outcast, he clings to old notions of right and wrong, with a conservative bias. He hates perverts, homosexuals, communists, liberals, smut entertainment, and thinks society is on its way down. Rorschach is obsessed with crime fighting in the filthy dark streets. He was bullied as a kid ("retard"), had no father, and was rejected by his mom, who was a prostitute. His identity is the mask, and he is tough as nails.

Wolverine

Fear/Desires: Want to be independent.

Motivations: Works alone and wants to have a little fun along the way, in order to feel content.

Important Life Events: Battle with the Hulk in the Canadian wilderness. Weapon X program giving him Adamantium-laced bones. Becoming a member of the X-Men. Constant battles with his brother Sabretooth. Falling in love with Mariko Yashida.

Reactions Under Stress: Capable of going into a berserker rage. Also known to disappear when he no longer wishes to be part of a team.

Mental Health Range: Wolverine is all over the range, but exists primarily in the 4-6 range of mental health.

The Wing Slider: Might have a weak 5-wing.

Instinctive Subtype: Sexual.

Quirks: Believes all the world is a stage, and can easily switch masks, so to speak, as needed. The Stranger by Billy Joel, another famous Type 4, expresses this worldview descriptively. Is also a man of mystery, which is a common trait among 4's.

Also Could Be: Due to his temper and gruff exterior, Wolverine appears to be a Type 8 to some.

Wolverine is the most popular X-Men character in Marvel Comics, and arguably the most popular Marvel character. It's easy to think of Wolverine as an Enneagram Type 8 because he's just such a rugged individualist who goes into a berserker rage and starts killing people when he loses his temper, but Wolverine is actually an Enneagram Type 4.

Here's the argument why: Wolverine prefers to be a loner, and doesn't want to lead. He'd rather sit back, criticize leadership, and work alone. When he's forced into teaming up, he's the one that complains or criticizes the leader, or simply walks out. Now sure, 8's can do that, but 8's always have a desire to actually control the team; Wolverine doesn't want to control the team. If his teammates are going to hang along with him, okay. That's fine, just don't get in his way. That's one angle that separates the 4 from the 8.

Another subjective quirk that shows that Wolverine is a 4 and not an 8, or any other type, is that he truly has an air of mystery about him. Other types are a little bit more revealing, except 5's, of course. Wolverine is Mr. Mystery, Dr. Mystery, and Supermystery. He doesn't even know his origins. That whole mysterious lover gimmick fits into the 4 type, as well.

He has had many lovers throughout the years he's been around in the Marvel Universe (he was born in 1882). The love is deep, the love is personal, and he doesn't judge based on race or religion or status. He just establishes a connection with someone. He can see an attractive element of someone, and he can go head over heels for a woman. In recent stories, women have thrown themselves at him. Examples of loving relationships include Silver Fox, Mariko and Jean Grey. He also has a bonding relationship with Storm.

He has this gruff exterior, where he seems like a womanizer and Mr. Tough Guy, "Let me open this beer, and I got hair all over my chest, and I'm smoking a cigar," but he truly has a warm heart under that hard exterior. This is another element of a 4.

Fours create images, just like Threes do, but they do it for different reasons. And it's another reason why this relates to Wolverine being a 4: iIt has to do with his identity.

Fours are like chameleons- not necessarily in a manipulative way, but in a way to "find themselves." Fours can act differently, more so than other types, depending on their environment. So, the same Four can be professional, withdrawn, quiet, and shy in one scenario, and then a passionate lover in another. In another scene, he can be a samurai warrior or soldier (like Wolverine). A Four can wear just about any hat he or she wants to put on. That's because, secretly, 4's believe that the world is a stage and we're all wearing masks. They can freely put any mask on that they please because it's all an illusion anyway. They just want to have some fun and maybe on the journey they can really find out something about themselves, so they can grow.

Wolverine *has* grown over the years. He started off as such a mean-spirited team member in the X-Men in *Giant Size X-Men* 1. He was someone who, frankly, as readers, we had no interest in. We didn't like his original yellow costume and he argued with his fellow X-Men. He didn't want to be a team player. He stood out as not being on the same page with Professor X or Cyclops, leaders we were conditioned to respect, in the original Uncanny X-Men comics. Yet, that's why other fans latched on to him: they like the bad boy and anti-hero.

The Undertaker from WWE started off as a villain in pro wrestling, became an anti-hero, and now he is one of the most beloved characters in wrestling history. The same goes for Wolverine, in terms of the way he worked himself up. First, he really started off as a villain or mercenary. He made his first appearance in *Incredible Hulk* 181 as a Canadian super-agent. Next time we see him, he doesn't want to join the X-Men, and he's kind of forced to do it, out of politics with Alpha Flight and the US government.

Then he just grows and grows and grows. We see that he actually has a heart, but is extremely tough. He is a hero that kills in self-defense with no regrets. It just adds up to a very total composite- a very human character that has every emotion in the book that he can tap into, at any given time. It makes for very interesting stories.

In terms of marketability, he is one of the most marketable in all of comic books. In the 1990s, he generated more money than any other hero. He is A-list. He has been featured prominently in the X-Men films and actually had his own film, with another on the way. Marvel believed that Wolverine can be on par with Spider-Man. Based on peak comic book sales and appearances, he's either more popular than Spider-Man or equal to him.

Wolverine's range is very wide, much more than 8's. Of all the types, 8's have to be one of the most one-dimensional characters- no offense to any of the 8's reading this, but 8's are very simple and straightforward .They want control over their environment or be the boss, whether they can see it or not. They want to be in control of their own destiny and their own comfort.

Wolverine shows a large spectrum of emotions and can function in different settings. He's all over the place. He has been all over the world and all over the timeline. He's been on many different teams, even the Avengers in the comics.

To us, there's no doubt that Wolverine is an average 4. Why is he average? Well, he can't control his emotions. Let's put it this way: he attempts to control his emotions through discipline, with eastern religions and philosophies. When his emotions get the best of him, and those emotions can be love or anger or anything, he goes into this berserker rage. He starts to try to deaden those feelings by drinking heavily and smoking.

He has these healing powers, so he doesn't suffer from any long-term effects of drug or alcohol abuse, or any binges that he participates in. You have to understand: it must be pretty weird to live 100s of years and keep regenerating so you can't die. So, he does things to survive that other people wouldn't.

Unfortunately, his life has been tough and filled with tragedy, which is another unfortunate sign of 4's that they get into. For Wolverine, he is just kept on the average, in that middle range. He can sometimes fall all the way down. Conversely, he can go all the way up, at times. Generally speaking, he is in the middle of the pack, in terms of his mental health, but he's an exception when it comes to being a strong character.

What we've learned:

- Fours are tough, and can be confused with Eights. Fours have warm hearts under the standoffish or rugged exterior.
- Fours are attracted to passion, excitement, and finding mates.
- Fours prefer to work alone, but over time can learn to deal with other personalities.
- Fours must discipline themselves to avoid the traps that lead to unhealthiness.
- Fours are tragic figures.
- Fours are well-rounded in the human condition.

Other Average 4's
Buffy
Buffy Summers [Buffy the Vampire Slayer] is misunderstood, intense, and emotional. She believes in self-improvement and self-discovery. She is heroic, despite being forced into her role as a superhero. At times, she is more concerned with her love life and romance than slaying vampires. She is a loner forced into a group, and not a natural leader- she expects others to follow her or get left behind, because she doesn't need anyone.

Oliver Queen
Green Arrow [DC Comics], a.k.a. Oliver Queen, started out as a billionaire protector of Star City. Eventually, he lost everything and became a socially-conscious hero for the common man. His 4-6 team-up with Hal Jordan in the 1970's DC Comics run is the stuff of legends. He uses trick arrows to fight crime. He has had a hot-and-cold relationship with Black Canary over the years. Oliver Queen is an unabashed supporter of left-wing causes.

Lisa Simpson
Lisa Simpson [The Simpsons] is your typical child Four prodigy: creative, sensitive, doesn't feel like she fits in, and questions authority and society. She's "human" and a little narcissistic at times.

Han Solo

The captain of the Millenium Falcon, Han Solo [Star Wars], along with his sidekick Chewbacca, are smugglers who get caught up in the war against the Empire when they are hired by Obi-Wan Kenobi to transport R2-D2 to Princess Leia. His rebellious streak is revealed often, like when he refuses to go along with plans or listen to reason. He is a compulsive risk-taker and gambler who won his space freighter in a card game with Lando Calrissian. Han has a soft romantic side, as well as a guilty conscience that betrays his bravado. He becomes jealous of the relationship Luke and Leia have until he learns that they are brother and sister. In the expanded universe, he ends up marrying Leia (a 4 - 8 marriage combination that we have observed to be fairly common in real life) and having Jedi children.

Aang
Unable to accept that he would be separated from his friends in order to complete his Avatar training, Aang [The Last Airbender] flew off on his Air Bison, Appa, and ended up frozen in ice for 100 years. Racked with guilt after discovering his disappearance indirectly led to the deaths of all his fellow airbenders, he becomes motivated to redeem himself, complete his training, and stop the Fire Nation from conquering the world. Aang becomes infatuated with one of his new friends, Katara, and loses sleep when worried he can't handle an upcoming challenge. He loves to pull pranks and joke around. Aang is a gifted airbender who eventually conquers all four elements.

Robert Barone
Robert Barone is Ray's older brother, and the oldest son of Marie and Frank Barone. He is a big, hulking man who works for the NYPD as a police officer. Robert constantly feels like Ray gets all the love and attention from their mother, and that Ray gets all the breaks in life. This inspired the title of the sitcom, "Everybody Loves Raymond." It's represents Robert's sarcastic view of Raymond, and a view of himself, that nobody loves Robert. He has sabotaged romantic relationships in the past with his quirks. He enjoys commiserating with Debra about Marie and Ray. His character does progress during the show, perhaps the only main character to do so. After 8 seasons, he finally marries Debra's best friend Amy and begins to feel the love that he's been looking for his whole life.

Number Six

Fear/Desires: To be free.

Motivations: Does everything within his power and ability to escape the Village and his previous life.

Important Life Events: Resigns from his job, and is abducted by a mysterious international group.

Reactions Under Stress: Take action. Yell. Stand up for his rights. Plot his escape.

Mental Health Range: 1 to 3. He is a man pushed to his limits psychologically, and still manages to stay true to himself.

The Wing Slider: Slight 3-wing.

Instinctive Subtype: Self-Preservation.

Quirks: Self-reliant, with a strong sense of his own identity.

Also Could Be: It's possible he is a Type 6, or perhaps a rugged individualist Type 8.

The Prisoner is one of the most unique (and cult) television shows of all time. It was the brainchild of Patrick McGoohan, who was famous for being Danger Man. It's hard to separate the character of Number Six from Patrick McGoohan. Number Six is a retired spy who is kidnapped and placed on an island with other people who "know too much." The society is skewed: it gives the captives the illusion that they are free because the prison is actually an island with a town. The keepers of The Village are led by different people called Number Two, who answer to the mysterious Number One. For Number Six, who actually is an Enneagram Type Four, it is the ultimate showdown of the man versus society theme. His captors want to know "Why did you resign?" Number Six will not cooperate.

Many Type Fours may not realize this, but their attitudes, beliefs, and actions subconsciously rebel against society. Fours are social critics, and can express their views by writing, art, acting, music, and other creative ventures. Most Fours want to be left alone. Many are loners or form intimate relationships with only a handful of people in their lives. Fours create their identities from the ground up, but unlike the fake images of Type Three, they do it in a quest for meaning in life or to determine their role in it. Fours tend to create their own mental prisons- they are their harshest critic and worse enemy. A Four who can accept who he or she is can achieve greatness and happiness.

On the surface, the goal of Number Six is to escape The Village, but *The Prisoner* is much deeper than that. The show has a metaphoric context, and this is confirmed with the last episode "Fall Out", which is an allegory. Throughout the episodes, Number Six uses his intelligence, willpower, and resourcefulness to resist his tormentors. He is secure with his identity and is disciplined. He doesn't "win" every episode, but he never gives up his information, although it could be argued he DOES- maybe there is no secret as to what led to his resignation; he just wanted to retire and relax. Maybe Number Six is in a Kafkaesque world for no reason! (Kafka was also a Four.) The entire concept, theme, and style of *The Prisoner* show and Number Six is that of a creative Type Four.

Number Six is a symbol of individuality, justified rebellion, self-reliance, and at the very basics, he is the old school everyman: a person who will not surrender rights to an oppressive government without a fight. Number Six is surrounded by people who did give up the fight, and they seem to be shells of their former selves. Number Six does not give up. He is inspiring.

Number Six's personality would change when Number Two would drug him in attempts to rewire his mind. This, along with Damian's professional background with prescription drugs, inspired Tony to create the concept of Enneagram Rewiring.

In the last episode, it seems that Number Six had created his own reality. In the end, he self-renews, as he finally obtains his freedom. Number One is revealed to be Number Six. This is an allegory for Jung's concept of a shadow- everyone has a dark side. Number Six confronts and overcomes his dark side, becoming a "person". Amazing how Patrick McGoohan subconsciously tapped into the Enneagram. Fours subconsciously defeat themselves, and the key to freedom is overcoming oneself.

Never before or since has a television show demonstrated the stages of personality development and social commentary as *The Prisoner* did.

What we've learned:
- Healthy Fours are self-renewing, disciplined, and break free from their self-imposed negative view of themselves.
- Comparing Spike, Wolverine, and Number Six, we can see that if a Four can be more at ease with himself, asserting control over his emotions and primal urges, the level of healthiness increases.
- Fours can explore parts of reality from their subjective existence that other types may never tap into.
- Fours can create something 100% unique and deep, unlike some creators who are hacks.
- We can learn much from a Four's personal experiences, as well as when they hold the mirror up to ourselves. Ignore their messages at your own risk.

Other Healthy 4's
Captain Picard

Captain Picard [Star Trek] is easy to misidentify because he acts so proper like a Type 1, but he is a 4 who integrates into a healthy 1, and always retains his healthy Fourness. Jean Luc has a heart, but manages with his brain. He is compassionate and creative, but also shy and reclusive (he retreats to his chambers to think). He is professional and performs his duties in a balanced way- healthy 4s can do that! He was wild when he was younger. His relationship with Riker is a classic Enneagram 4-6 teamup.

Part Five
Type 5

Lex Luthor

Fear/Desires: To prove he is competent.

Motivations: To receive praise and admiration for his intellect and inventions.

Important Life Events: Lab accident costs him his hair. Kills an alternate version of himself in Crisis of Infinite Earths. Forced Superman to break the rules and turn back time to save Lois Lane.

Reactions Under Stress: Vengeful. Talks his way out of trouble.

Mental Health Range: 6 through 9.

The Wing Slider: Has a slight 6 wing.

Instinctive Subtype: Self-preservation.

Quirks: Cares a great deal about imperfections in his physical appearance. The mad scientist.

Also Could Be: Many online think Luthor is a 3 or 8 because he is a business leader.

In an IGN poll, Lex Luthor was voted the fourth greatest villain in all of comics, while Wizard magazine voted him the eighth. Both missed the mark.

Luthor, who is as recognizable as the Joker to casual fans, is the most revered, respected, and capable villain within the fictional DC Universe. He's been around for 72 years, and is regarded as the mastermind behind the major plots in the DCU. His personality and design has changed over time, although it seems to be coming full circle. He starts off as a mad scientist in *Action Comics* 23, whose strength was his brain. He builds giant robots, weapons, loves to rob banks, and create sinister plots to destroy Superman and rule the world.

His Silver Age version added a new depth to the character. In *Adventure Comics* 271, Luthor is an up-and-coming scientist in Smallville and was going to use his powers for good. However, he blames a lab accident, which caused a fire that seared his head, on Superboy. So, yes, he loses all his hair and then becomes one of the greatest super-villains of all time.

This may seem crazy to you, but many Enneagram Type 5's that we have interviewed have a self-conscious quirk about their hair or other perceived physical deformity or inferiority complex. This is similar to Type Fours who believe that they are flawed or "missing something".

Some Type Fives that we know do not desire any attention to their toupee or wig. We have to pretend it doesn't exist. They're very sensitive about that. It's not just hair; it could be anything. It could be a chip in a tooth, or a pimple, or even a mole.

With Enneagram Type 5's, everything is in their mind. Their physical attributes, the exterior, is a second-class citizen in their world-view. Therefore, anytime an imperfection arises in their physical body, it adds to their skewed notion that they are, somehow, inferior or incapable, or do not measure up to other people. It gives them the green light to explore other realities and fantasy worlds.

This fits Lex Luthor perfectly. The Silver Age and Bronze Age Lex Luthor (1960 to the early 1980s) is fueled by his hatred of Superboy/Superman simply because of that lab accident which cost him his hair. After creators Marv Wolfman and John Byrne revamped the character in *The Man of Steel* 1 as a CEO/businessman/Donald Trump type, Luthor's main motivation for hating Superman is that Superman was beloved and adored by Metropolis, yet Luthor was not.

So on one hand here's Luthor, the businessman, one of the richest men in the world, who has created so many jobs in Metropolis and is a well-known philanthropist. And here's Superman, an alien, that comes and gets all the attention. That gets to Luthor, big-time.

When we add the fact that Luthor was dating, or trying to court, Lois Lane, and then Superman shows up and Lois goes gaga for him, well, that adds to the inferiority complex that Luthor has.

Some may think that Luthor is, say, a Type 3 or a Type 8, but the truth about his personality type comes down to the basic fears and desires. Lex Luthor wants to prove and show to the world, Lois Lane, and himself, that he is capable and competent. It's not about control, and it's not about a false image. It is about competence, and for him to prove to himself that he's a big man- the smartest man in the world, the richest man in the world, the technological genius of the world, and the world's savior. Overcompensating much? The modern version of Luthor publicly states that he wants to make the world a utopia, and he is even elected President of the United States (a major story arc, with a key issue being *Lex 2000* 1).

Although 8's are very clever, and 3's are Machiavellian, Luthor is the master schemer in the DC Universe. His plans last for years, and that shows you the raw power of his mind, and the minds of Type 5's. Luthor planned his presidential run by acting generous after Gotham City was devastated by an earthquake in *No Man's Land*. They're cerebral, innovative, secretive, intense, and isolated. In the Golden and Silver Age, Luthor always escapes jail; he will always think of a plan to get out. It doesn't matter if Superman takes all his weapons away, he will think of something.

Some of the modern day treatments of Luthor truly tap into his evilness, as an unhealthy Type 5, and focus on man versus superbeing. Generally, we as readers like to sympathize with non-powered beings going up against an unbeatable foe, but with Luthor, well, he's the powerless individual, and Superman is the ultimate power-being. It's an interesting take on the dynamics.

Luthor actually has a big similarity with Satan. They're both narcissistic, proud, charismatic, self-confident, and they think they are capable to lead humanity. It's even more ironic when, in *Action Comics 900* (which, in our minds, could have been the last issue of Superman), Luthor gets the power of God and actually is a benevolent God, but his one problem is his hatred of Superman. That is his final undoing.

Luthor is one of the most complex fictional characters in comic books and any medium, truthfully. Although there have been many different takes on the character, including alternate versions, reboots, and retcons, at his core Luthor is the calculating mastermind villain, as opposed to the brute strength or psychotic foe.

What we've learned:
- Fives are prone to being cerebral.
- Unhealthy Fives are dangerous to others.
- Fives are sensitive but don't like to admit it, and may overcompensate or escape.
- Fives have an innate aptitude to discover, build, investigate, or research.
- Be prepared to suffer revenge if you cross an unhealthy Five- it could happen years from now.
- Fives can be trapped in a fantasy world.
- One key in typing fictional characters, famous people, or those you know is to get to the root of their motivation and fears. Use the Enneagram books or websites as a reference and narrow it down to prove it. It's the best way to dissect someone who acts like a mean boss- Eights don't have a monopoly on being dictators.

Other Unhealthy 5's
Doc Samson

As Bruce Banner's psychiatrist, Doc Samson [Marvel Comics] sought to cure Banner from transforming into the Hulk. In the process of draining the Hulk of gamma radiation, Samson succumbed to temptation and dosed himself, turning into a super-powered being with green hair. He went on to woo Betty Ross, which led Bruce Banner to douse himself with gamma radiation again. A completely untrustworthy medical professional who is unapologetic about manipulating others. He appears to be good at times, only to double cross others for selfish reasons.

Loki

Loki [mythology, Marvel + DC Comics] is the God of Mischief. He is an introvert that likes to work from behind the scenes with master plots. Here is a controversial opinion that we at the DailySkew hold: Fives aren't all shy, quiet, and socially inept. In terms of scheming, not even 3s and 8s can out-think Loki. He is the Trickster archetype, who causes strife just for the heck of it, but tends to back down from confrontation. Loki is the absolute master of lies and a known traitor.

Evil-Lyn

Evil-Lyn [Masters of the Universe] is a cold, cruel, and serious sorceress dedicated to studying and perfecting arcane and dark magics.

Extremely powerful, she joined Skeletor's legion of evil for her own secretive reasons, which have to do with her father. Manipulative and plotting, she resents Skeletor, who is a Type 8, but she serves him nonetheless- until the time is right to overthrow him.

The Leader

The Leader [Marvel Comics] lost his humanity due to gamma radiation, and is a skewed Type 5 with that big brain of his. Too smart for his own good, he is not grounded in reality, and his obsession with the Hulk and Bruce Banner has lead to much death. The master plotter and schemer of the Marvel Universe, his plans last years.

Drusilla

Drusilla [Buffy the Vampire Slayer] is an insane Type 5 who is no longer grounded in reality. There's something to be said about being a schizophrenic psychotic depressed delusional **VAMPIRE**- it's a place of torment that unhealthy Fives can descend to. She plays things hot and cold with her boyfriend Spike, and seems to take joy in manipulating his emotions.

Reed Richards

Fear/Desires: To discover and learn.

Motivations: Conducting experiments and research at his laboratory for the good of mankind and to satisfy his curiosity.

Important Life Events: Attempted to warn Victor Von Doom about the miscalculation in Victor's experiment at college. Leading a space mission with his best friend Ben Grimm, along with Sue and Johnny Storm, to investigate cosmic rays. Forming the Fantastic Four. The birth of his son Franklin. Discovery of unstable molecules and The Negative Zone.

Reactions Under Stress: Reed tends to turn inward and think of a solution to problems that come up. Socially, Reed is inept and can be awkward when dealing with the public or Sue's needs.

Mental Health Range: Reed Richards is in the average health range for his type (4 to 6), while occasionally tapping into the healthy range (1 to 3).

The Wing Slider: Reed Richards has a medium 4 wing, which explains his creativity in the lab.

Instinctive Subtype: Self-Preservation.

Quirks: Being awkward when around Sue is a reflection of a typical quirk for male Type 5's, who tend to have difficulty in romantic settings. Also, fives are the archetype for professor and mad scientist characters.

Also Could Be: N/A.

Reed Richards is Mr. Fantastic, the de facto greatest mind of the Marvel Universe, and leader of the Fantastic Four. He is Marvel's first science hero, and he ushered in the rebirth of the superhero genre in 1961, with his appearance in *Fantastic Four* 1.

Yet he is, ultimately, an average 5. We would say that, many times, he's at a healthy level, but he does slip to the early stages of unhealthy when things go bad with his relationship with his wife, Sue Richards. On the average, he's an average Five.

Reed is the archetype of the absent-minded professor. He is not only a scientist who is extremely knowledgeable, studious, and analytical, but unfortunately he also loses himself in the work. He can be antisocial, and he'll drop down in the levels of healthiness all the way to being secretive and dishonest.

His relationship with Sue is very revealing as well, in terms of him being a Five. He is totally inept around women, although the occasional writer will come and have him with a beautiful long-lost love that he met in college (Alyssa Moy, as shown in *Fantastic Four* Vol 3, #5 in 1998). Reed is generally shy and inept around women- they're just not his thing. Females are still a mystery to him because relationships can't be measured in statistics or numbers, so it's not in Reed's playbook. Reed does have a romantic side, but it's usually exposed only when Sue shows her frustration. Sue (Enneagram Type 2) needs attention and will act out if she feels neglected.

Reed gets distracted by his scientific work; he likes to investigate and discover new things- that's his main motivation. Some of his body of work includes rocket science, extra-dimensional travel, discovery of the Negative Zone and Microverse, and unstable molecules. There were times in the 1970s, after Franklin Richards was born, where Reed really wasn't that involved in Sue and Franklin's life, or they have differences of opinion. He's just too focused on some project that he's been working on. In *Fantastic Four* 130, Sue leaves Reed over Franklin. Generally, though, he'll do anything to protect them. The problem is that his mind is usually elsewhere.

In terms of optimism versus pessimism, Reed can swing, big-time. He has this idealistic altruism that science can cure all the perils of mankind, and he can discover the true nature of reality to benefit humanity. On the other end, the pessimism, if we can label it as such, is that he sees everything in numbers. So he can come off as being cold and calculated. Since he takes away the human aspect of a story or an event, it may seem like he's being a downer, but in his mind, he's not depressing. In one example, in *Fantastic Four* 243, Mr. Fantastic saves the life of a dying Galactus- a god-like destroyer of worlds- even though he knows Galactus will kill again because Reed deems that one life is invaluable and that Galactus is a necessary part of the universe. Again, the debate wasn't if Reed should take initiative and *kill* Galactus, it was if he would *let him die* due to injury. Therefore, using Reed's mathematical formula, one life of a being who is guaranteed to kill again is worth more than billions of lives.

The only time Reed truly loses his cool is if his relationship with Sue becomes damaged. It could be an argument where he pushes her away, such as during Marvel's *Civil War*, when Reed was on the side of pro-registration with Iron Man. He had believed that superheroes should register with the government, be supervised and under control, whereas Sue respected the privacy of super heroes. That split them, to the verge of separation. In the end, Reed took a shot to protect his wife's life.

Without Sue in his life, and this has been shown in the regular Marvel Universe and the alternate realities, Reed totally becomes imbalanced. According to the Enneagram, Fives disintegrates into Seven. Reed will become totally reckless, as he'll become consumed in his work and start taking huge risks, without care for his life. So, he has a suicide run aspect to him when he loses Sue. This is seen during their first separation, *What If The Invisible Girl Had Died?*, Civil War, and stories where Sue is not around. Reed will invariably stop shaving.

Another huge aspect of Reed's character is his relationship with Ben Grimm, The Thing, his best friend (and Type 7). He feels guilty that Ben became a monster. After all, Reed is the one that gets Sue, Ben, and Sue's little brother Johnny into an unprotected space ship, and they get bombarded with cosmic rays. The three of them receive cool super powers, but Ben becomes a rock monster. For years and years, he's been trying to cure Ben, and there are a few occasions where he does, but, comics being comics, Ben will always revert back to the Thing.

In *The Thing* 23, it is revealed that Reed knew that Ben *always had the ability* to back into human form at will, but Alicia Masters loved the Thing, not Ben. So, psychologically, Ben put a mental block in his mind. Yet Reed didn't tell Ben this back in the day. That is an example of Reed withholding information.

In a famous mini-series *Fantastic Four vs X-Men*, it was implied that Reed knew the cosmic rays would have transformed all four people into super heroes, yet didn't tell his crew. That story turned out to be a plant by Dr. Doom; it wasn't a true diary, but it sounded like something Reed would do. It totally fit his personality. Average Type Fives play it loose with the truth. They come off as being so dependable and logical, like a Type 1, that it's easy to think they're honorable and they're always going to be upfront with you, but when they lie, they do it with such a straight face that you wouldn't think twice about it. With Reed, it seems like every storyline he's covering something up, such as in John Hickman's modern storyline "Future Foundation", where Reed teams up with Reeds from other dimensions without telling his family. That's why we put him as an average 5.

In the realm of fiction, it's easy to say, "Well, this person dedicated himself to being a superhero. So he must be healthy, because he's altruistic. Average people just don't go out and sacrifice their lives to save humanity." Well, that's not the way we rate things. You can just look at the Enneagram orange textbook called *Personality Types* by Don Richard Riso with Russ Hudson, and in the appendix there is a chart with levels of development. You can see that, even if you're very charitable, even if you, on the surface, have a great family life, even if you are a police officer or a firefighter or a doctor or a soldier, where society says, "Oh, you must be a hero," you can still be average. You can be unhealthy. You can be anything on that list, depending on your stress levels or spiritual path. That's just the way personality is. Personality is a mask.

For Reed Richards, he is a flawed hero. Sure, he always comes out on top at the end, but there is tragedy there, all because of his lying, his obsessiveness, and his, truthfully, lack of humanity at times.

In recent years, with all the decades and decades of stories, Marvel has hired good creative teams that remember all those stories. They try to make Reed evolve. Even as Reed evolves and grows, he still not healthy all the time. He's still making deals with other versions of Reed Richards from other dimensions, he has secrets with his daughter Valeria, and he's keeping that information from his wife, Ben, Johnny, and Franklin. He no longer has qualms about teaming with Dr. Doom to combat a greater evil (like an alternate version of Reed- as seen in various FF series in 2012).

Reed Richards is a double-edged sword: a genius and a master of all sciences, yet someone who can't figure out how to talk to his wife.

What we've learned:

- Fives have issues with the opposite sex and socializing in general.
- Fives can get lost in their research or hobbies.
- Just because fictional characters are heroic, it doesn't mean they are healthy on the Enneagram scale.
- Fives have a unique form of logic that seems outside of the box. It technically holds up in consistency, but can leave other types baffled with its priorities, which usually take away the human element.
- A Five and Two couple is bound to have issues, as the Two requires high maintenance and the Five requires "private time".
- Even though Type Sevens can be master strategists, when paired with a Five, the Five is the logical one who is looked to for advice (see X-Files: Scully and Mulder).
- Mr. Fantastic is light-years ahead of Lex Luthor regarding morality and spiritual development, but Reed can be deceptive. He also practices the "ends justify the means", which usually has controversial consequences.

Other Average 5's
Bruce Banner
Bruce Banner [Marvel Comics] is one of the smartest men in history, an expert in physics, mathematics, robotics, and actually everything-except psychology to help his tortured soul. Banner is socially inept, isolated, and fears rejection. Of all the major Marvel heroes with their neuroses and tragic edge, Banner has been the most suicidal, due to his curse of transforming into the Hulk when he gets angry. Fives don't like to get angry; they prefer to think their way out of problems. Poor Bruce.

Dr. Manhattan
Dr. Manhattan [DC Comics] could be a cold, logical, computer-like Type One, but the DailySkew believes he is a Type 5. His whole angle is observing the true nature of reality. He was already a scientific genius, and as a God, he had mastery over the timestream, energy, and matter. That being said, his fear of rejection was still there, as were his problems socially, dealing with women.

Dwight Schrute
Dwight Schrute [The Office] is a nerdy kiss up office worker. He is an average Type 5 that isn't actually that intelligent, he just "looks" smart. You may have had co-workers like Dwight. What's a Five without intelligence or perceptive talents? A lame troublemaker, tattle tale, weird, antisocial, and mischievous Five. Dwight is into sci-fi and fantasy, a staple

of Five tastes.

The Watcher

The Watcher [Marvel Comics] truly doesn't need any explanation: he observes, is rational, cold, and doesn't like to interfere. He's a collector, historian, and likes the obscure. He ... watches. In Earth X, he becomes obsessive, cruel, and without a healthy body.

Scully

Fear/Desires: She loves to investigate. Afraid of being incompetent.
Motivations: Get to the truth using scientific methods and evidence.
Important Life Events: Chose to become an agent, not a doctor. Being assigned to work with Fox Mulder. Death of her father.
Reactions Under Stress: Early in the series, would be overwhelmed by facts and fail to act. Later on, was tough and willing to do what was needed.
Mental Health Range: Always a relatively healthy, stable character who grows during the series. Scully lives in the 1 to 3 range.
The Wing Slider: Slight 4-wing.
Instinctive Subtype: Self-Preservation.
Quirks: Tends to be shy around the opposite sex, and prefers to dress conservatively.
Also Could Be: Her use of logic might indicate she is a type 1.

Dana Scully of the *X-Files* was one of the strongest women portrayed on television in the 1990s. Scully is portrayed at the beginning as a Jodie Foster/*Silence of the Lambs* behavioral FBI agent. That was her core being, and then she evolved. Scully is not just a direct copy, even at the beginning, because she is hyper-critical of her partner, Agent Mulder, who is the paranormal expert. Anyway, Scully was the thinking heroine, as opposed to a generic sex symbol.

Scully is a medical doctor. She is highly intelligent but is a product of the school system that doesn't encourage non-scientific or non-statistical analysis. That means Scully always had problems making leaps of faith or assumptions that Mulder was able to reach. She didn't have the instincts. She was always by-the-book and highly skeptical.

The thing with Scully is that she's conservative, kind of boring, and kind of shy. She is not on the same page with Mulder. She always questions him. Even in the face of evidence of a UFO or a monster, she still won't make that jump to believe in the paranormal. Mulder easily makes that leap. In fact, he already committed to that conclusion beforehand.

You may think, "Oh, she's a 1, right? She's just a logical freak of nature. She's going to be critical. That's a 1 thing, right?" Well, as we've written with some other characters, types don't *own* specific emotions or traits. Let's compare the 5 versus the 1.

Ones have a set of logical beliefs/methods. It's like a word game with them. If they create the parameters of a problem or follow a set of rules handed down by an authority figure, they'll strive to abide by that. Sometimes they get hypocritical, but they're going to attempt to follow those rules rigidly, and apply that to how they perceive the world.

The Five starts to develop their perception of reality at a young age. So they might be into ancient Egypt, who killed JFK, fantasy novels, comic books, or baseball statistics. They get fixated on it. They'll devote their lives to learning everything about it, becoming an expert on it. Truthfully, when faced with evidence that is contrary to their belief, they're actually going to reject it. A very typical 5 is someone that calls in a radio show at 3am and talks about aliens, or ancient Atlantis people who live in the center of the earth and are communicating with Nazi UFO ships from Venus. That's not the majority, but perhaps they are the statistical mean of 5's. They have a belief and changing their mind on it is hard. On the internet, it's easy to spot a Five: they can create hundreds of detailed pages on an obscure topic or ramble four hours on a podcast or video about it, without care for entertainment value.

The One, although they may give you the impression that they don't change their minds, actually will change their minds and just pitch it so that they do not appear to change their minds because they don't want to give the impression that they're flip-flopping. George W. Bush is the perfect example of a 1 who does hypocritical things but always pictures himself as someone who is steadfast and doesn't change his mind.

Going back to Scully, she doesn't fit the parameters of a One. Based on her belief systems, she decides to choose the route of science over anything else. Even in the show, although she starts off being Catholic, she had been so absorbed in medical school and then as an FBI agent, doing autopsies and forensics, that she kind of lost her way a little bit, in terms of not going to confession anymore. She still had a very strong faith in Jesus or God. She always wears and displays the cross. She always defaults back to a belief in God, but it's only when her dad dies and she encounters a crazy fetish serial killer that she goes out of her way to visit the church regularly. Episodes which focus on her religion are "Miracle Man", "Beyond the Sea", and "Lazarus".

Although there were some contradictions there in terms of her religious faith, they are realistic. Millions of people have the same conflicts. Whereas Mulder did not believe in God, Scully was able to make that leap of faith. It is the only leap she makes; everything else has to be proven by science. So, that was a very interesting parallel that Scully and Mulder had.

Mulder is a Seven- a Sherlock Holmes and Batman Type 7. He's able to see your footprints and know where you were and know what school you went to. Crazy stuff like that. So they had a very interesting relationship (no romance).

First and foremost, Scully is an investigator. She's very objective. However, in the first two seasons, she is blind to Mulder's, and the viewers', conclusions. The viewers see what is going on. We're looking at the monsters. We're putting the pieces together with the government conspiracies. The first couple of seasons, Scully will analyze evidence. She'll put it through her computer. She'll take samples. She'll do all the examinations but she won't come to the same conclusion that Mulder and the viewers do, even when it's obvious. She just misses an actual smoking gun or denies things.

When first introduced, Scully had a FBI Academy chip on her shoulder, acting as if she's fresh out of the Academy and idealistic, whereas Mulder seemed much more experienced about the real world.

We understand why the writers had to do it, but it was frustrating at the beginning. The good news is her character really grows when she starts to experience the conspiracy, the aliens, the military and the cover-ups. Then she is right on board with the viewers and Mulder. It's a great team. They're no longer squabbling at each other, which used to make the viewer frustrated when they argued.

Scully is always healthy throughout each and every season, even though she didn't come to the same conclusions as we did. Who cares? That has nothing to do with mental health. She is always alert and insightful. She has compassion, and was extremely knowledgeable. She was a little stuffy, but that's your choice, you know? That's not an issue of personality healthiness. She usually dressed down on the show. She also seemed shy around men, which is a trait of many 5's, fictional and nonfictional. They just have an aversion to the opposite sex or same sex, depending on how they go there.

That being said, I would say early on, in season one, Scully may have been sometimes shown as a little intellectually arrogant, as well as argumentative, a little too much. Sometimes she'd be overwhelmed by facts and just stop, instead of taking action, but those instances were few and far between.

Toward the end of the series we see the evolution of her character. She becomes an icon in the UFO community because she really takes Mulder's mantle and runs with it. She is more outgoing, although she always had been tough.

You could say that Scully is book-learned, whereas Mulder is totally practical, at least when they start off. Then, Scully becomes the ultimate agent because Mulder always had the self-destructive aspect of him, like many 7's have. In the end, he pretty much disappeared off the face of the earth.

Anyway, the 5 and the 7 tag-team is pretty hard to beat because they're both cerebral. Sevens are prone to action and the Five is prone to getting all the necessary data before acting. So, if they actually can come together, which they did, they're going to uncover conspiracies and stop the bad guys. They're going to crack down on criminal activity and whatever monsters are roaming around. When you are talking about the raw intellect of Scully and Mulder, you're talking about a near-invincible tag-team, and definitely one of the most important and memorable relationships shown on television, in terms of a man and a woman in law enforcement.

What we've learned:
- Fives are fantastic researchers.
- Fives preach logic, but their logic is different than Ones who also preach logic. Generally, a Five will work off preconceived notions or experiences and then use the facts to support it. Ironically, Scully calls herself a skeptic but in fact is close minded to the paranormal, even when the only conclusion can be an out-of-the-box explanation.
- Fives are the most shy of all the types. This doesn't mean they don't socialize, it just means they are prone to being withdrawn and introverted. They have to learn how to express their thoughts into words, and get over the fear of rejection.
- Fives and Sevens can get on each other's nerves because they are on opposite ends of the Enneagram: the Seven lives off physical excitement while the Five loves mental stimulation. That is not to say the Seven doesn't like cerebral exercises or the Five doesn't like to have sex- it is their default disposition to handling problems or being under stress. The Seven will take action and the Five will think about it.
- A healthy Five is at ease with herself and has no fear of rejection or perceived flaws. She can be fully integrated into society and be respected by her peers for being honest, correct, quick thinking, and also compassionate. Healthy Fives are virtually unbeatable in fiction because they are so efficient and all-knowing.

Other Healthy 5's
Giles

Rupert Giles [Buffy the Vampire Slayer] is a textbook intelligent Five who is into books, the obscure, and dabbles in arcane magic. A mentor, he had difficulty being challenged by his emotional student Buffy. Giles was the technical support and leader from the side-lines of Buffy's team- not really an active and physical participant. A very valuable Five, he used his knowledge to help battle evil. Shy and reserved, he stuttered around women and girls.

Morpheus

Captain of the Nebuchadnezzar in the real world, Morpheus [The Matrix] is a wanted terrorist in the Matrix. We see his healthy self-confident side as he leads Neo down the rabbit hole and reveals the truth to him. As the onion layers are peeled back during the trilogy of movies, we learn that Morpheus has a tragic romance with Captain Niobe (acts awkward around her), as well as a rivalry for her affections with Locke, who is the commander of Zion's military forces. He does not take orders from Locke seriously, and the only reason he remains a captain is the faith the High Council has in him. We also see his beliefs challenged, as Neo reveals there is no guarantee Zion can be saved. In the midst of this crisis of faith, after losing his ship and learning that the Oracle is simply a program from machine world, Morpheus' efforts over the years are finally rewarded when the machines agree to peace with the humans, thanks to the person Morpheus had freed from the Matrix and believed in.

Sorceress

The Sorceresses [Masters of the Universe] is a powerful magic-user who is He-Man's and Man-at-Arm's guide. She protects the secrets of Castle Grayskull, and lives an isolated and lonely life, as she is tied to the castle itself. Known to withhold the truth (she's Teela's mom). She is a force of good, but will do anything to protect the castle's powers from evil (Skeletor, Hordak, and King Hiss). The Sorceress can be physically overwhelmed.

Part Six
Type 6

Parallax

Fear/Desires: Fear of losing his loved ones and those he protects.

Motivations: To save the lives that were lost when Coast City was destroyed.

Important Life Events: Mongul wiping out Coast City. Killed the Guardians and others in his attempts to bring back Coast City. The discovery that the Parallax took over Hal Jordan during this time.

Reactions Under Stress: Snaps and becomes homicidal.

Mental Health Range: 8 to 9. Totally unhealthy.

The Wing Slider: Weak 7-wing.

Instinctive Subtype: Social. Wants to bring others back to life.

Quirks: Flipping out after the loss of someone close is common among fictional sixes.

Also Could Be: Geoff John's concept of Emotional Spectrum shows Parallax as being a demon, and links the color yellow to fear, and Sinestro is a symbol of fear as well. So there could be an argument that Parallax could be an embodiment of a One.

Hal Jordan is the Silver Age (1960s) version of DC's Green Lantern character. This version of the character has the most loyal following. He is a 6w7. Becoming Parallax in 1994 was one of the most controversial storyline decisions made by DC comics of all time. Hal Jordan's fall from grace actually fits in with Sixes, and how they react under severe stress and tragedy. All his life, Hal Jordan has displayed a complex personality. Although he is the noble, self-sacrificing hero, and for many years he was a trooper because he listened to the Guardians of the Universe, who are basically average Ones and Fives (who are very impersonal and logical), Jordan finally flipped out.

Damian Hospital read every Green Lantern comic ever published, so this analysis of Jordan comes from an authority. Hal just couldn't take it anymore. This was with the years of buildup, with him going head-to-head and arguing with the Guardians many times in the 1970s and 1980s.

However, one of the reasons why this storyline was so controversial was because Jordan actually was a super healthy 6 who integrated into a Nine. This was when he had the white sideburns, which showed his experience. In fact, under writer Gerald Jones, he was an ambassador for the superheroes- a wise and experienced superhero that the other heroes went to for advice. Jordan was very comfortable in his own skin and showed a lot of personal initiative and responsibility. In other words, he grew up and didn't act like the brash young hotshot who shied away from duties.

So, it was a surprise at the time to comic book readers when he totally went crazy, but it's still in the Enneagram Type 6 text book. His city, Coast City, which he defended for decades, was totally wiped out by a villain called Mongul; seven million civilians were killed.

Jordan believed that he could remake or undo the damage. He went to the Guardians and they, of course, rejected interfering and he, pretty much, killed them and anyone who got in his way. Is that a stretch? Well, many fans thought so, but you have to understand the mind of an unhealthy 6: it's all about attachment, injustice, and they get overcome with grief and guilt. That's exactly what happened to Jordan.

Does it make any sense? From the Enneagram point of view, it does. We wish fans in the 1990s had access to the Enneagram, because this topic was a huge hot button.

Do we think that the writer Ron Marz was a hack? Hack is a strong word and it wouldn't be fair to attack Marz like that. DC wanted changes and he delivered; he wanted to start anew with a new Green Lantern. Because sales were low before he came on-board, he and DC blew up the old. Do we think that DC did this for sales? Yes, without a doubt. But, technically, the fall of Jordan is in the realm of possibility. Also, we have seen this happen with Willow from *Buffy the Vampire Slayer*, who is also a 6, when she becomes a dark witch after her girlfriend dies.

So you can see the pattern of what happens to a 6 when tragedy occurs.

The Joker is an interesting version of the 6, as well. The Joker is a 6 in The Killing Joke by Alan Moore, but a 7 in most other renditions. As the Six, you can see that he's a struggling comedian just trying to put food on the table. His wife dies absurdly (defective toaster), and he totally gets desperate and flips out. So, this flipping out mechanism is part of the 6 textbook.

Parallax's later appearances (*Zero Hour* and *Green Lantern* comics featuring Kyle Rayner) feature him trying to restart the universe in his own image, where everything is back in the Silver Age, everyone is alive, and everyone is clean cut. And that really shows you that 6's have this skewed and insane attachment to the past and this idealized version of the world. That's what Jordan displayed under the influence of Parallax.

Let's put it this way: if you happen to be an Enneagram type 6 who is hopefully average or healthy, or maybe even integrated into a Nine, and you're reading this, just imagine if a tragedy happens in your life that is unspeakable, and you actually had the power to reverse it or punish the person or thing that caused that tragedy. If you can imagine such a scenario, then you can imagine what happened to Hal Jordan when Coast city was wiped off the face of the earth. He was powerless to do anything about it, and his bosses, who he served for 35 years (in comic book publication history) refused to assist him.

Later revisions by writer Geoff Johns have Parallax being the god of fear- in other words, the yellow impurity of the Green Lantern battery. This was a retcon that was created to salvage Hal Jordan's character. In other words, Jordan didn't snap. The yellow impurity, which is the Parallax demon, went into his mind and took him over. This also can be proved as being a logical explanation because Jordan is prone to mind control. In earlier comics, from the Silver Age to Bronze Age, Jordan's mind was stolen or he wasn't himself a few times. So, that is within the realm of possibility from DC Comics, but it is a cop-out to make Jordan unaccountable for his actions.

That being said, fear plays a major role in 6's lives. Under stress, 6's can be seen to be fearful of authority, suspicious, and they make other people scared, too. Sixes are usually very solid and reliable citizens. However, when they start to go under stress, some of them start to get self-disparaging or panicky. Everyone that they had inspired in the past starts to totally lose faith, not only in the 6 but in humanity itself. You respected a hero but now he's acting all scared and cowardly. That's what fear is.

Therefore, even with the retcon of Parallax taking over Jordan's brain, that still fits the way an unhealthy 6 acts: he is overcome with fear and becomes fear itself.

Therefore, even though for some fans, Hal Jordan becoming Parallax doesn't make any sense, in the realm of the Enneagram, either with the original storyline of Jordan snapping, or with the Parallax god taking over his mind as fear, both fit in the unhealthy 6 Enneagram textbook. Parallax is a perfect example of what happens within a good trooper when things go very badly.

What we've learned:
- Sixes may establish themselves as troopers or heroes, but they may react horribly under tragic circumstances if there is a slow buildup of issues in their lives that goes unaddressed.
- Sixes are obsessed with justice, injustice, fair play, and expect payback from authority figures, especially if they put in good work.
- Sixes have a love/hate relationship with authorities, and once they lose patience, will take authority in their own hands.
- A Six can be very patient, passive, obedient, and take a lot of abuse, but one day there will be a straw that breaks the camel's back. With Jordan, Willow, and The Joker it was a major tragedy. In reality, Andrew Joseph Stack III was a Six who flew his plane into an IRS building. He had posted a manifesto against the government, big business and the tax system. The software engineer and musician had said the IRS took his savings away.

- Unhealthy Sixes feel completely justified with their actions, so they become dark mirrors of their "nice person" image.

Other Unhealthy 6's
The Joker
Batman's arch-nemesis, The Joker [DC Comics] represents virtually everything Batman hates. One origin story shows him concluding life is a joke after the seemingly meaningless way his wife died (as depicted in Batman: The Killing Joke by Alan Moore). The Joker hysterically laughs in highly inappropriate situations, which is a quirk among some sixes we've observed. Sadistic. He loves inflicting pain, and creating Faustian choices for his enemies. The Joker uses unexpected "gags" and tricks to defeat his enemies and instill fear. The clown face is an exaggeration of typical unhealthy six behavior, tending to show a smile while raging inside.

Merman
Mer-Man [Masters of the Universe] was a hard character to type, but ultimately we determined he is a Six based on his loyalty to Skeletor and empathy he had to Beast Man. Additionally, he abused his power as King of the Sea, lost his kingdom, and is forced to work for Skeletor [Type 8]. That's bad luck, and that's a Six.

Spider-Man

Fear/Desires: Fight for justice due to feelings of guilt over the death of his Uncle Ben.

Motivations: Protect loved ones and the public at large from evildoers so that the world can be a just, safe place.

Important Life Events: Bitten by a radioactive spider. Raised by his aunt and uncle. Let a thief go free; moments later, the thief shot and killed his Uncle Ben. The Green Goblin killing his first true love, Gwen Stacy. The marriage of Peter Parker and Mary Jane Watson.

Reactions Under Stress: Will initially withdraw, quit, and throw his super suit in the garbage, but eventually comes to his senses, rebounds, and fights for what's right.

Mental Health Range: Peter Parker has been at the top of the healthy range and at the bottom of the unhealthy range. Due to editors at Marvel Comics wanting to keep Peter perpetually young and inexperienced, he remains an average type, in the four to six range of healthiness.

The Wing Slider: Has a slight 7-wing.

Instinctive Subtype: Social.

Quirks: Has a tendency to under-think. Can swing from friendly to anti-social at the drop of a hat. At his best, can be a self-sacrificing, inspiring hero.

Also Could Be: N/A. Peter Parker is the quintessential Type 6.

Peter Parker the Amazing Spider-man is an icon in comic books. Spider-Man is a multi-faceted individual and arguably, the most popular and identifiable character in Marvel Comics. He's also an ultimate Six. He's an average 6 because he's always been marked with an inferiority complex for being a nerd, and is consumed by guilt.

Under original creators Stan Lee and Steve Ditko, in his high school and college days, he's a wallflower. Peter doesn't think he's that good looking and he's marked by the tragedy of the death of his Uncle Ben, which he feels responsible for. It's hard to be healthy when your main motivation is guilt

Peter Parker is the textbook 6 in that he under-thinks. Now, granted, he's a genius. He has a high IQ, but he still is slow on that chessboard when it comes to thinking multiple steps ahead. That winds up creating situations that cause him a lot of distress.

Yes, being a 6 has a lot of contradictions. For example, he may have excellent agility and spider sense that warns him when something bad is going to happen, but he seems accident prone at times, falling all over the place, i.e. "bad luck".

He also swings from being antisocial to friendly. "Your friendly neighborhood Spider-Man" was also in a title called Marvel Team-up, and is now a member of the New Avengers. Spidey has been shown to team up with all sorts of heroes, yet, ultimately, he has the aura of being a loner. It's a paradox. Welcome to the world of 6's. It's hard to label them, and you don't want to keep your mind closed and underestimate them because they are very unpredictable.

You can also tell that Spidey is a 6 based on his relationships with other characters. J Jonah Jameson, publisher of the Daily Bugle, hates Spider-Man with a passion and abuses Parker. Parker tries to please him. This mirrors the 8 – 6 relationship. Helen Palmer wrote about the 8 and 6 relationship in her famous book, *The Enneagram at Love and Work*, which is phenomenal in that any 6 who reads that will see that it's just like the script from his or her life when it comes to dealing with an 8 in an authority role in their lives.

Uncle Ben is a 9- the gentle, kind, good, stable role model in Peter Parker's young life. He is someone who had loved Peter unconditionally, who was a family man, and worried about him a little bit. Ben is an older integrated version of Peter (Sixes go to Nines), but for the most part the teenage Peter ignores Ben's advice, and is a bit whiny.

Aunt May is the moral compass. She is a strict Type 1. That's where Peter gets his ethics and morality from, but like all 6's, they have to learn on their own. He had two great role models, but when we first see Peter in *Amazing Fantasy* 15, he makes the wrong decisions.

When Peter Parker gets his powers of being a spider, he abuses them. He becomes egotistical with them. He becomes a TV celebrity and even defeats Crusher Hogan in a pro wrestling match, and ultimately didn't think that it was his responsibility to capture a thief when a police officer said, "Stop! Stop!" Not his job.

Of course, that thief went on to murder Uncle Ben. Thus, Spider-Man dedicated his life to protecting innocents- out of guilt.

Parker can swing from being dependable, likable, expressive to falling all the way down and being the exact opposite. He can be worried and mulling, unapproachable and very defensive. His Daily Bugle co-workers in the comics would say he is unreliable, but with good intentions. The reason is that he's trying to juggle many different things in his life. Do you know any 6's like that in real life?

It's very hard to judge a 6 at times because they come off as troopers: nice guys or nice gals. When you first meet them or if you know them casually, they appear to be drama-free. They appear to be good citizens that follow rules and comply, but with Peter Parker, he has issues with authority. He hides behind his sarcasm when he makes jokes while he fights. He is a walking neurotic hero. A therapist would have a field day with Peter Parker/Spider-Man. Of course, he has saved numerous lives and the world countless times, so it is what it is.

Perhaps the most frustrating thing about Spider-Man is that anytime he shows any emotional or spiritual growth in the comics, the writers or the editor-in-chief will scale him back to acting like a rookie. So, he perpetually is learning on-the-job. One of the things that frustrates us severely is when a 6 forgets the skills or lessons he or she has learned in life. That's what separates, in our opinion, stable 6's from unstable 6's.

If you look at a real life Six, such as the Yankees pitcher Andy Pettitte, you'll see he's a veteran now and he has learned how to pitch over the years. He has learned how to focus, and perfected new pitches and strategy by mixing his pitches up. He's learned how to perform under pressure and to block distractions out.

When comparing the 2009-2012 Andy Pettitte to the rookie Andy Pettitte, or even Andy Pettitte in his prime, when he was 29 years old, winning awards and championships, one of his peers, David Cone, said, "This older version of Andy, although he may not have that fastball anymore, is actually the better version of Andy." With Spider-Man, and some 6's we have interviewed in real life, they are the opposite of Pettitte in that they completely forget the things they learn.

Now we're not just talking about how to run a machine or a computer program. We're actually talking about dealing with co-workers, bosses, and spouses. How many 6's do you know that are on their third marriage or have issues with authority figures and everyday responsibilities that we all have? It's like everyday is new to them.

Peter Parker still can't hold his photography job with the Daily Bugle and still has girlfriend issues, even though in 1987 he was married and had a stable relationship with Mary Jane. He still can't make inventions and sell them for millions of dollars in the Marvel Universe. Even if he's with the Avengers, he still comes off as being like a joker. So he's still not a respected leader in the Marvel Universe.

He's still going through those things. Even when there are changes made by a new creative team or editorial decision, he gets reverted back. The excuse you may give is "Well, it's episodic. It's just a comic book showcasing serial adventures of a fictional character. They can't grow. The Simpsons always have to act like that." Actually they don't *have* to stay the same and other comic book characters grow, evolve, age, or at least change since their first appearance.

We don't buy the theory that every generation must experience a Peter Parker that is still learning how to be a hero. Batman doesn't learn how to be a hero. He always comes off as being a distinguished veteran of the game. Even if they scaled-back Batman's age to being 27, the man still acts like he's in his 40s. The same goes with Superman. If DC wants to show Superman being young, they're just going to call him Superboy or make him slightly rash. Yet Spider-Man has a slow learning curve.

Green Lantern is a perfect example of a Six that grows in comics. The younger version of Green Lantern was so cocky, arrogant, and close minded. Over the years, he learns how to grow and learn from his experiences, and apply those experiences. That doesn't mean he can't be cocky anymore, but it does mean that he looks himself in the mirror and knows why he's cocky. He knows his deep issues, yet he perseveres and overcomes them.

That's something Spidey doesn't do. Instead, he gets scaled back to the wet-behind-the-ears kid. Anything he says gets misconstrued, especially when he tries to repair his reputation in the Marvel Universe. This mirrors the bad luck 6's have with communicating.

Sixes are detailed. They'll go on and on and on to make sure you get the story right. Sure enough, either you weren't paying attention because they rambled or, even though they were so detailed, they still couldn't communicate what they were trying to say. You may get angry at them, or if you corner them and say, "You really said, 'X'" they're going to turn around and defend themselves. They're going to become an apologist. They're going to parse words, avoid saying anything offensive to you, and be polite because.they're good guys or gals..

Damian has read every single issue of *Amazing Spider-Man* and we can vouch that Spidey is an average 6. In fact, every 6 could read any issue of Amazing Spider-Man and really understand the Enneagram.

Let us just throw some adjectives at you about Peter Parker/Spider-

Man. In terms of his level of mental health, he's been healthy- no doubt about it. When Spidey is on and in the zone, he can be secure, positive-thinking, and decisive. He is likable, obviously loyal, and bonds with others.

However, Peter overcompensates. A man who is so optimistic suddenly becomes cynical. Spider-Man can lose his temper for no reason, just because he had a bad day. He can get depressed because he opened the refrigerator and there was just sour milk in it; he had forgotten to buy food, or he didn't generate enough money to buy food. We've seen Spider-Man become helpless, emotionally needy, humiliating, and self-punching.

Parker has issues with authority, and he doesn't realize it, but wonders where the anxiety comes from. The amazing and spectacular thing about it is, according to Don Richard Riso and Russ Hudson's *Personality Types*, the lowest level of health for a 6 is when a 6 drops out and hits skid row, and becomes guilt-ridden, tormented, and self-hating. That's scary because Parker has done that many times. He's thrown his costume into the garbage pail. If he feels that something bad happened to Mary Jane or Aunt May, he will hit that level and he'll get reckless. He's a very complex character that can function at unhealthy levels.

If you want to compare him to Superman, it's a perfect way to see the difference between Marvel Comics and DC Comics. Superman never falls down anywhere close to those unhealthy levels. The worst that Superman gets is that he's condescending.

Peter Parker is one of our favorite characters and there's a reason why he is on Marvel comics A-list. Spider-Man represents the common man-someone trying to pay bills, go to school, and take care of his family. He's been doing it since 1962. He won't give up, and that's inspiring. Hopefully we'll become inspired and never give up.

Spidey will make sacrifices to help others and is a deliverer of justice. He likes to correct injustices to prevent tragic things from happening to people; he is a hero, through and through. We believe that Stan Lee and Steve Ditko were tapping into the tragic hero from Greek mythology when they created this character.

What we've learned:
- Sixes try to juggle different parts of their life with mixed results.
- Sixes are sensitive, defensive, reactive, and try to do the right thing.
- Sixes are prone to forgetting/blocking events or are gullible and overly optimistic, which causes them to "repeat" similar situations.
- Sixes are walking contractions and can swing from optimism to pessimism, passiveness to aggressiveness, being trusting to suspicious, complying to rebellious, and sociable to isolated.
- Sixes are prone to being consumed by guilt and justice.
- Some keys to a Six becoming and remaining healthy are to learn from his or her mistakes, to focus their priorities, and be responsible with their duties and relationships, instead of wandering around, looking for adventure at a whim.
- Sixes make great apologists and defenders.
- Some Sixes make jokes and sarcastic remarks to cope under stress.

Other Average 6's
Frodo
Frodo Baggins [The Lord of the Rings] is an unwilling hero who is cowardly, confused, has bad instincts, and wide-eyed. It was frustrating for healthy Sixes to watch this famous hero in the movie theaters!

Original Blue Beetle
Blue Beetle [DC Comics] loves to makes jokes while fighting, has no real super powers yet wants to fight crime, and is super-smart. This joker was never appreciated until he died as a martyr.

Cyclops
Cyclops [Marvel Comics] is an uptight, nerdy, and square Six. He is the field leader of the X-Men. He's really uncool, and secretly battled inner demons which focus on doubting his ability to fill the shoes of Professor X, doubting Jean Grey's love, competing with Wolverine, and being an outcast with his mutant eyes. A very unlikable Six in the early X-Men comics and movies since he is the establishment.

Dr. Crusher
Dr. Beverly Crusher [Star Trek: The Next Generation] is the Chief Medical Officer for the U.S.S. Enterprise-D. She has conflicted feelings for Captain Picard, whom she loves but also blames for her husband's death. Beverly tends to be a bit overprotective of her son, Wesley, and

not listen very well. Dr. Crusher likes to complain about not having a solution before having an "A-ha" moment that solves the problem. She is moral and principled, and believes saving a life is more important than Starfleet Regulations.

Regular Hal Jordan
Green Lantern (Hal Jordan) [DC Comics] is a high-risk adventurer Type 6 who wanted to follow his dad's footsteps as a hot shot test pilot. Haunted by his dad's death, Jordan became reckless: alcohol + ladies. Accepting his fears allowed him to grow into one of DC's most powerful and noble heroes. Was a trooper but constantly butted heads with his bosses, the Guardians of the Universe, and quit or was fired several times.

Nite Owl
Nite-Owl [DC Comics] isn't a confident hero, but he is intelligent and a do-gooder. Based on Blue Beetle, he is very similar, but has a bigger gut- literally- that shows he gained a lot of weight over the years. Part of yet another famous 6-4 team-up with Rorschach.

Willow
Willow Rosenberg [Buffy the Vampire Slayer] is a bookworm. She is nerdy, gullible, naive, shy, and a loyal best friend. She and Buffy make a great 6-4 team-up. Willow became a magic user, and flipped out when her girlfriend was killed.

Chief Engineer Scott
James Montgomery Scott, or Scotty, as he is affectionately known by Kirk and others, is in charge of engineering on the starship Enterprise. Scotty is obsessed with and attached to his ship. He believes the Enterprise is the best ship in the fleet, and will defend that point if his ship's name and integrity are besmirched, especially by Klingons. Scotty displays a full range of emotions throughout his appearances, including the poignant scene when he carried his injured nephew unto the bridge of the Enterprise during Star Trek II: The Wrath of Khan. He loves to joke around and needle his captain. He frequently complains when he thinks Kirk is pushing the ship too hard, and likes to play by the rules. However, Scotty is very capable of coming up with creative, outside the

box solutions to seemingly impossible problems. We decided his character most closely resembles a type 6, but it is possible that he is another personality type. The characters on Star Trek: TOS, outside of the big three (Kirk, Spock, McCoy), got very little screen time and very little development. In real life, actors like James Doohan and Walter Koenig had to fight to get lines to say on the show.

Ensign Chekov

Chekhov was introduced during season two of Star Trek: TOS as a navigator and a science expert. The show producers brought him in to attract the teenage market to the show, stylizing his hair and look to mimic the Beatles and the Monkees. HIghly intelligent, he would man the science officer station while Spock was on an away mission. As a character outside of the big three of Spock, McCoy, and Kirk, Chekhov's character did not get a lot of development during the original series. The one episode where he played the central character, he was visited by an old flame from Starfleet Academy who attempted to manipulate him into helping her but failed to do so. Chekhov received more of a central role in the movies, in particular Star Trek II: The Wrath of Khan, where his loyalty to Kirk was on full display. He refused to shoot his old Captain, despite being under the influence of a worm wrapped around his cerebral cortex, controlling his actions, and the voice of Khan urging him on. It should be noted that Chekhov might not be a 6, but perhaps a 4. Again, due to the lack of characterization on the original series, his personality type is more debatable.

Captain Marvel (Shazam)

Fear/Desires: *To be good.*
Motivations: *To fight injustice and help others out with his amazing powers.*
Important Life Events: *Meets a wizard who gives him the power of the gods.*
Reactions Under Stress: *Throughout most of his history, he maintained a positive attitude under fire.*
Mental Health Range: *Lives in the healthy range of one to three.*
The Wing Slider: *Slight five-wing.*
Instinctive Subtype: *Self-Preservation.*
Quirks: *Shazam has had several bouts of bad luck in the real world, including having to change his name, being jobbed out by Superman, and the tastes of audiences changing just as he was given a fair shot. Bad luck is definitely a Type 6 quirk.*
Also Could Be: *Shazam originally was a Superman clone, meaning he started off as a Type 3. Billy Batson has, up until DC new 52, always been a positive, optimistic Type 6.*

Captain Marvel. Billy Batson. Shazam!

One of the most recognizable characters in comics, Shazam, we're sorry, *Captain Marvel* always plays second fiddle to Superman. We're going to compare them in a moment, but first let's go over that little slip of the tongue.

Captain Marvel is one of the most misnamed characters in comics. Casual fans call him Shazam because most of his comics were called Shazam, and he says, "Shazam! So, finally, in 2012, DC comics decided to rename the character to Shazam, just to clear up any confusion.

Now, let's talk about Shazam's personality type: if you were a child of the 1980s, and you read *Justice League International*, (and shame on you if you did not read Keith Giffen's and DeMatteis' work) you would've noticed that Captain Marvel is shown as being innocent. He is pure, moral, Mr. America, dependable, humble, positive, optimistic. He is such a healthy caricature of a superhero.

We're so used to Peter Parker being neurotic, Batman being obsessive, X-Men being outcasts, Iron Man being arrogant, and the Hulk being a rampaging lunatic, that it is refreshing to the writers of this book to come across a character like Shazam, who has no mental hangups. Billy Batson/Captain Marvel, a.k.a. Shazam, is in a class by himself because for some reason, after the baby boomers, Generation X gravitated towards characters like the Punisher, Wolverine, Ghost Rider, and the aforementioned heroes that have huge character flaws. (In the movies, it was Freddy and Jason. In pro wrestling, it was the Road Warriors).

Without a shadow of a doubt, I think society would be such a better off place if everyone emulated Captain Marvel, instead of worshipping "hero celebrities" that have huge issues with being role models, and have questionable ethics and morals. Captain Marvel is one of the most responsible action-orientated heroes of all time.

He always plays second fiddle to Superman. This is, very simply, the reason why: Fawcett Comics created Captain Marvel because DC, or National Comics at the time, had Superman. So, they said, "Okay. Let's do Superman, but let's just change it a little bit. We'll call him 'Captain Thunder' and his powers will be from the gods. Instead of being Clark Kent, he can be a kid who turns into Superman. Kids should buy that."

Well, kids loved it. They loved it so much that DC, or National Comics, had to bring Fawcett Comics to court. They had to settle, and sure enough, that began the misidentification of Captain Marvel as

Shazam. They couldn't use Captain Marvel in the title of the comics. They finally went out of business. Then, DC bought the rights to Captain Marvel, thereby gaining control of both properties in the 1970's.

Sure enough, Shazam 1 sold like hotcakes, but it was the 1970's. Society had changed. DC did a pretty good job of "jobbing out" (another wrestling term) Captain Marvel so he always looked like number 2 or 3 to Superman, and sales declined. By then, and on to the 80s, 90s, 2000s, and now the 10s, there's just so many heroes that emulated Superman. Captain Marvel now gets lost in the shuffle. That shows you the bad luck quirk that Type 6's have made a name for themselves- the whole Charlie Brown or New York Mets thing.

Bad luck is not exclusive to Sixes but it is a major theme of their type. DC has always tried to launch a Shazam comic. It just always runs out of steam. There's just something that goes wrong, each and every time, and the character seems to be relegated to team books or being used as only a guest appearance.

It could be because there were so many other Captain Marvel variants running around, such as Mary Marvel and Captain Marvel Jr., Uncle Marvel, that talking tiger, and the actual wizard Shazam. The modern stuff tried to simplify things, but it eventually got confusing. This takes away from the core character. Superman has his Superman family, too, but he doesn't need Supergirl, Krypto, or even his parents. He doesn't need that stuff to work. I don't think Capt. Marvel needs it either, but they keep putting them in there with him anyway.

Let's get back to Marvel being a healthy 6. Look at all the characteristics of a healthy 6, and it's all Captain Marvel. He's hard-working, he's a martyr, completely trusting, and ever vigilant. He can connect to anyone. Cap is trustworthy, and unlike Peter Parker, who can't make his mind up and is filled with self doubt, Captain Marvel does make decisions. He is self-affirming and grounded in reality. Green Lantern (Hal Jordan) is a Six who only *wishes* he could consistently tap into that healthy level that Captain Marvel is at.

Here is the other thing that is not in any textbook about the

Enneagram: Type 6's have that wide-eyed, everything-is-new, childlike perception of reality. In other words, to a 6, everything is new, and newer is usually much more exciting. It is a revelation to them. They get pretty enthusiastic about something. They may have experienced something twelve times in their lives, but to a 6, it's as if it was the first time.

So, they truly love experiences. That could get them in trouble sometimes, which may make you wonder about them. Do they remember anything? You can look at it from that negative point of view, but the flip-side is that they can take enjoyment and they can see the best in every experience. It could be the latest movie, which really might be crappy but to them it's like the first movie they ever saw. Of course, I'm being slightly tongue-in-cheek, but you get the idea.

Take famous broadcaster John Sterling, who is a Type 6. If the Yankees rally, he will say, "That was the greatest win that I ever saw. The was the greatest comeback in Yankees history." Of course, just last week he said the same thing!

Healthy Type Sixes can really get the most out of life by enjoying it so much, whereas on the bottom end of the spectrum, a 6 that sees everything as new will take that literally. So, a 6 may forget how to drive, forget how to use a PC mouse, or forget what happened yesterday. This quality could be good or it could be bad.

Some trivia: Captain Marvel, from the 1980's until fairly recently, was not two different personalities. Billy Batson, the kid, was a boy in a man's body, while the golden age Captain Marvel was two distinct personalities- Billy Batson transforming into Superman, the ultimate 3. Yes, he was a direct copy, but Batson himself was always a 6 who strived to be optimistic, even though life isn't fair to him. He persevered.

In DC's new 52, Captain Marvel was not introduced as one of the first 52 titles, and I said, "Man, is he getting jobbed or what? How can you not have a Captain Marvel comic book for rebooting the DC Universe?" Then, around eight months later Billy Batson appeared in the back-up story of JLA. Interestingly enough, the back-up stories were actually better than the main story in JLA.

So here we have the New Age Billy Batson. What do you think DC did to Billy, the ultimate, pure 6? Well, they show you his origin and let's just say that, instead of maintaining his spirit of gullibility, trustworthiness, doing the right thing and being a model citizen for kids to follow, this new version of Billy Batson is like an orphan from Craigslist. He's deceptive, lies, gets into fights, has a victim personality, has a chip on his shoulder, and is angry at the world. Is he a 6? Well, if he is, he's an unhealthy or immature one. Or maybe he's totally different.

Captain America is a man out of time in the Marvel Universe because he was around during World War II. In the DC Universe, Captain Marvel always acts like a man out of time because he's a kid in a man's body. So, all the adults around him, like Batman, Superman, Wonder Woman, Flash, Aquaman, Green Lantern, Hawkman and all those other JLA heroes look at him and they're like, "Are you serious? Why are you saying, 'gosh'? Why are you saying, 'holy moley'?"

It's amazing, right? Captain Marvel is truly a golden age character. He is one of the most recognizable characters in American history, even though he got jobbed out so many times. Everyone knows that symbol, and everyone knows what the word Shazam is, even though they may not know where it comes from. Shazam!

He acts like he's from the 1940's. Yeah, it's kind of weird. Kids don't act like that anymore. He has that "man out of time" feel to him. He has that child-like gullibility and naivety to him, and he really stands out. Otherwise, he'd just really be a Superman clone if he had the aggressiveness or subtle arrogance that Superman has. If he was universally recognized by the DC heroes as being "the world's mightiest mortal", (which is really just a tagline. In practice, DC has never really treated him like an A-lister in the DC Universe) he'd be Superman. But he's not Superman. He's human. He's a 6.

What we've learned:
- A healthy Six is known for for being moral, righteous, and ethical.
- Sixes view experiences as new. This is a double-edged

sword; although this creates excitement and wonder, the drawback is that the Six may not learn valuable lessons.

- Sixes act more human than Threes.
- Sixes are gullible and trustworthy. The healthy Sixes are shining lights.
- Sixes are attracted to martyrdom.

Other Healthy 6's
Optimus Prime
A self-actualized Type 6, Optimus Prime [Transformers] is the leader of the Autobots in their war against the Decepticons, and in their struggle for survival. He is willing to sacrifice his life for his followers and those he has sworn to protect. He never gives up. Optimus is an inspiration to all who stand with him, and is able to overcome insurmountable odds single-handedly in battle. He has faith in those on his side, and abhors evil in all forms. He was so loved by the fans that he was resurrected by popular demand after falling in battle against Megatron in the first Transformers: The Movie cartoon from the mid 1980's.

Will Ryker
Will Riker [Star Trek] is a Six that manages with his gut, instincts, and experience rather than Starfleet regulations. He enjoys making personal connections, especially with the ladies. Ryker loved the security of being his captain's (Type 4) right-hand man, as opposed to having a ship of his own, and the added responsibility. He valued stability over ambition. Ryker is suspicious of aliens he did not know.

She-Ra
She-Ra [Masters of the Universe] is a pure, noble, responsible, morally correct, perfect Six who is compassionate and always does the right thing.

A saint, she was originally brainwashed and very loyal to Hordak, and made a vicious Force Captain (company woman) before the mind spell was broken.

Part Seven
Type 7

Q

Fear/Desires: To relieve boredom.

Motivations: Acts out in order to relieve boredom.

Important Life Events: Several encounters with the Star Trek: The Next Generation crew, including one where he became human for a time.

Reactions Under Stress: Moody. Lashes out. Over time, he has grown and learned to get along with the crew of the Enterprise.

Mental Health Range: 5 through 8.

The Wing Slider: A straight 7.

Instinctive Subtype: Social.

Quirks: Real life unhealthy 7's that we have met will do crazy, irrational things. Never put any kind of behavior past a stir-crazy Enthusiast.

Also Could Be: Since Q is modeled after the trickster god archetype, it is easy to conclude that he is a Type 5. A deeper analysis reveals that Q is a 7, in our opinion.

Although Q from Star Trek is based on the trickster god archetype, such as Loki from Norse Mythology, their personalities are different. After much thinking and analysis, we have determined that Q is an Enneagram Type 7. The main reason is because of his infantile nature; Q is just bored. He has the power of a god, but has a short attention span. He acts out and does reckless things just to get a charge out of himself- thrills and mischief. This is a staple of unhealthy Type 7's.

No matter what they do, they believe that happiness comes from the outside: physical, external adventures. That's the essence of Q. He can pretty much do anything he wants. What does he do? He picks on humans or other alien races, just to make their lives miserable. We hate to say it, but that's what unhealthy 7's are all about. There's no doubt that Q is impulsive and irresponsible. He does things just to get a quick laugh. He likes when the humans play tough with him.

Q is very moody. It's amazing that such a powerful being can be so moody, and not have control over his emotions, but it's true. He s a manic-compulsive, and he will do anything in order to feel something.

Q views all living things as toys for him to manipulate, and he gets bored very easily because time has no meaning for him. He is very annoying to the crews of the various Star Trek shows he appears on. He was based on the character of Trelane, from the original series, a god-like infant who was also lonely.

Unhealthy 7's that we met in real life do the most perverted, risky, irrational acts that you can imagine. Never put anything past an unhealthy 7 when they're feeling a little stir-crazy. They're very hard to marry, and they're very hard to work with at times. Their minds are very chaotic. The healthy 7's, of course, have studied discipline and can focus that unlimited energy. Someone like Q, however, has never learned that discipline.

His character has grown over the years, of course. He once became human, lost his powers, and actually had a working relationship with Janeway from Voyager. And, in one of the best Next Generation episodes of all time, he actually helps Captain Picard look back at his life. He has learned and he has grown a little bit, but he's not someone you can trust.

The argument against Q being a Type 5 trickster or manipulator is that he's not behind the scenes. Q is just way too extroverted, even more than a Type 8 or 3. He's a super-powered joker. If you went into his mind for one minute, you'd be driven insane.

He doesn't like to be alone. Fives, on the other hand, like to be alone and are withdrawn. The Enneagram Type 7 likes to be among people. The loneliness will consume them, and for Q, well, he loves to bother the stuffy-shirted Captain Picard and the professional Riker, and the other crew members, because they provide him entertainment. For Q, the loneliness goes away when he entertains others, even if he risks killing them or sending them to the Borg, he doesn't care. As long as he gets excitement and thrill out of it, it is acceptable to him. That's what an unhealthy 7 does.

Average 7's deal with that same situation and hopefully they don't do things that are truly damaging their lives or relationships. But never underestimate an unhealthy 7. They're just so unpredictable, and at times self-destructive. The 7 also has similar traits to that of the 8 and the 3, or the narcissistic 4, in that they like to be worshipped and adored. Sevens don't like to follow orders. They're always questioning. Q is the master of his own destiny, but he answers to the Q Continuum, and he doesn't like that.

All the signs point to Q being an unhealthy Type 7. He is a great example of it and he is one of the most iconic villains in Star Trek, if not the number one villain in all Star Trek universes, due to his powerful personality and fantastic rivalry with the professional and serious Picard and Janeway.

What we've learned:
- Sevens believe the key to happiness is external, and not within themselves. Therefore, they need to be active, physical, around people, and shy from mental quietness. Drama is OK with them because it invigorates them.
- Unhealthy Sevens are prone to bullying, mischief, and addictions.
- Sevens don't like to take orders, and prefer to be in control of their own lives.

Other Unhealthy 7's
Galvatron
When Megatron was abandoned by the Decepticons and discovered by Unicron in Transformers: The Movie, he was remade into Galvatron [Transformers]. He was no longer the Type 8 who had fought Optimus Prime to the death; he was now an unstable Type 7 scheming to usurp his new master while regaining control of the Decepticons. Where Megatron suffered fools, Galvatron immediately displayed homicidal and vengeful tendencies with the murder of Starscream. He got rid of the stooges of the previous regime and replaced them with Cyclonus and an elite fighting force, all supplied by Unicron. In the end, his plan to destroy Unicron and the Autobots failed. He was tossed into space by Rodimus Prime, condemned to b-list status in the Transformers Universe.

Homer Simpson
A donut-eating worker bee who constantly endangers the lives of the community with his careless work at the local nuclear power plant, Homer Simpson [The Simpsons] comes home and promptly neglects the needs of his wife and kids. A terrible role model for Bart and Lisa, he is the head of a stereotypical American dysfunctional family. Exaggerated for comedic effect, nonetheless, Homer rarely displays any redeeming qualities and is usually displaying unhealthy tendencies. For example, he drowns his sorrows in beer, food, and television. Homer numbs out and only reacts when pushed to the limit.

Jack Bauer

Fear/Desires: To prevent the destruction of his homeland.

Motivations: Will do whatever it takes to prevent a terror attack from occurring, because that's his job.

Important Life Events: Joined CTU, wife killed, daughter disowns him, prevents nuclear bomb detonation, forced heroin addiction, forced to kill his boss, betrayed by lover, fakes death, imprisoned by Chinese, tortured terrorists, testified under oath to defend himself, retired to help African kids, running from the government.

Reactions Under Stress: Can be quick-tempered and pushy.

Mental Health Range: Jack has been enlightened and suicidal at various times during the series.

The Wing Slider: Possibly a weak 6-wing.

Instinctive Subtype: Social.

Quirks: Tends to be a workaholic who ignores the emotional needs of his family. This is common amongst type 7's.

Also Could Be: Action heroes tend to be type 7's or type 3's. It is possible he is an Achiever type.

Jack Bauer from the TV show *24* is the classic prototypical action hero. An action hero is usually an Enneagram type 7 or type 3, and some subgenres use type 8 as the rugged individualist. Sevens and Threes as action heroes, on the surface, are similar. Well, let us explain why Jack Bauer is a Seven, as opposed to a Three.

First of all, Jack Bauer, America's last hope against terrorism, doesn't care about his image. His motivations are to protect his country and his family from terrorists from any country. He will do anything, by any means necessary, to fulfill his duties and obligations to the president. The president is the only person that Jack listens to.

He values his job more than anything else. He lets it consume him. Threes do that; they're workaholics, but the motivation is different. Average Threes like to create, be the boss, or inspire others. Ultimately, they do this in order to be worshiped. We know that sounds offensive to average Threes, but they do create this image and are motivated to force others to support that image. They trick themselves into believing that image, and they impose that image on others to give themselves power.

Jack Bauer does none of that. Jack actually carries his sins with him. He has the ability to look deep inside himself and feel guilty about some of the things he had to do in the line of duty. Jack has a soldier's mentality, and he lost part of his soul in some of the covert actions, murders, and even torture he had to perform in duty for his country.

Jack is industrious; he has that Macgyver aspect of him, where he can get out of any trap, escape any situation, or solve any puzzle with the power of his pragmatic mind.

The TV show *24* and Jack Bauer are underrated in fiction and popular culture. *24* was consistently one of the top-rated shows in the world. The program would go up against some science fiction genres and reality shows to pick up the 18 to 35 male demographic.

For some reason, Jack and *24* were criticized a bit for the format, and of course, Jack was a conservative during George Bush's reign of eight years. Some people didn't like that.

Getting back to Jack being a 7: generally, he's quick-thinking, constantly under stress, and he lives for the thrill. There are times that Jack retired, but he always comes out of retirement due to his family or close loyal friend being in danger. Of course, things spiral out of control and he gets signed on full-time.

At one point, in one of his retirements, he did some missionary rebuilding work in Africa. That was one of the few times he felt content and didn't think of himself, because he was giving to and pleasing others. He was out of the rat race.

Jack swings from healthy to average to unhealthy, even suicidal. Jack, when under stress, is very demanding, pushy and insensitive. He gets jaded. He's a rogue. He doesn't march under the same orders as his co-workers and demands to be an exception because of his exceptional work. After all, he happens to be the most efficient government worker in the history of the US government. He's also extremely versatile.

We've seen many 7's that are future oriented. Many 7's that we know in real life have *specific* dates, timelines, and goals, based on when they hit a certain age, or a certain year occurs, or their children reach the age of 18. It's all part of their master plans.

Jack is constantly busy, and that was one of the jokes and criticisms of the show. You never see Jack just having a sandwich, or resting.

Jack was addicted to drugs one season after an enemy injected him with it. Jack continued taking them to escape from all the sins and pressure he had to deal with, being a super soldier. Many famous 7's in fiction were addicted to something. Sherlock Holmes is perhaps the most famous, and many characters that mimic Sherlock Holmes have some sort of addiction to alcohol, drugs, gambling, or women. Batman is addicted to crime-fighting.

Jack is completely unpredictable, and is totally out of control when things go bad. He is also heedless, truly death-defying, and numb. He went on many suicide runs in all the seasons of *24*.

His intentions were always good. Now the key to him being a Seven is that he would feel guilty about his actions afterwards. It's like he was compelled and obsessed when an emergency occurred, and he had no choice. This mirrors Batman and his war on crime- it's just not normal.

Their intentions are good but ultimately they become completely self-destructive. That is the road to depression and suicide runs; Sevens will create their own hell with their actions.

Another reason why Jack is a Seven is because he's so attractive. No, we're not talking about physical attractiveness alone. Sevens, no matter what they physically look like, have the ability through their confidence and charm to get the opposite sex or same-sex to be really attracted to them. Sevens have that aura around them where they're aggressive, and say what's on their mind, and make jokes (Jack was more serious since he was usually being tortured). But they have that sure-headedness confidence level and forward thinking. In fact, they overthink. So they know what you're thinking before you say it. They can project those things. Greg Maddux, the famous baseball player, who was probably the most shy and laid back Seven ever, had the ability to know what the hitters were thinking before he threw his pitches. He was also able to look forward three, five, or six spots in the batting order to know what the situation would be.

Those are the special talents and abilities of a Seven, almost to the point of being supernatural when it comes to predicting or anticipating how people will react. So, when it comes to attraction, a Seven, no matter how ugly or average physically they may be, have the ability to sweet talk you. They just have this whole, "I'm doing something, I'm so busy, I'm so important," aura that people viewing Sevens get caught up in. Others see their lives and want to live through them. Most people, hate to break the news to you, have boring lives. They work nine to five, they come home, they have their responsibilities, they read a book or watch television, surf the web, go to sleep, and repeat it for the next four days. Someone like Jack Bauer, and other 7's, are just so larger than life that they just have a cult following- they are an instant attraction.

Jack is an anti-hero, there's no doubt about it. Sevens have that anti-hero edge to them. They don't play things by the book when things get tough. They have little respect for authority, and even when lectured, they're going to go ahead and rewrite the rules themselves. They believe they are so irreplaceable that they can't get fired. They know they're going to get called back, or they know that they can do something on their own.

We rated Jack as average because he's so variable, but we do have to give the writers of *24* credit, and Keifer Sutherland, whose input into the Jack character was unbelievable, especially since he is a 7 himself in real life. The character grew and evolved. The TV show finished well. There were consequences for his actions.

Yet, since the fans demanded they continue the series even when the finales wrapped everything up nicely, sometimes the writers had to undo some consequences and had to set Jack back a little bit. In later seasons, Jack would act like he was not under stress; he'd act enlightened before he truly had to act. He wasn't as quick-tempered or pushy as he used to be.

Of course, there's a balance between being joyless and spiritual. Basically, at the end of *24*, Jack becomes truly free, spiritually. Jack had problems with women throughout the seasons. He seemed happy but he was always committed to his work. We see that in 7's in real life, as well. The mentality behind it is that they have to work to support and take care of their family, so they will neglect the emotional needs of their family, and that's it. There's no way around that. They don't even try to juggle it or balance it, like other personality types do.

What we've learned:
- Sevens are action-orientated.
- Sevens are unique leaders in that they can be judged by the bottom-line, as opposed to style or rule-following.
- Sevens leave little time for family due to their professional roles. It is not out of selfishness all the time; most of the time it is because they feel being a workaholic will safeguard their family's future. Additionally, Sevens don't like to be bored or tamed, and fear the homelife may take away their adventurous spirit.
- Sevens have the uncanny ability of foresight, but can be overloaded with the possibilities and not act.
- Sevens are moody.
- Sevens are extremely charming when they want to be.
- Sevens have issues with authority figures and are prone to stereotyping groups (including male/female behaviors).

Other Average 7's
Black Cat

Felicia Hardy [Marvel Comics] is an average 7 who exhibits unhealthy behavior when it comes to her relationships. She has an on-again, off-again thing with Spider-Man, and has trust issues with men due to being raised to be a cat burglar, as well as being raped in college by a boyfriend. Black Cat strives to be the best cat burglar, except when she is trying to prove she has good in her to Spider-Man. She has been known to seek revenge for perceived betrayals.

Mr. Incredible

Bob Parr [Pixar] is a super-hero in hiding after costumed vigilantes were outlawed by the government. Bored by his menial insurance job, he listens to the police scanner with his fellow former super, Lucias Best, a.k.a. Frozone. Bob eventually gets duped, falling into a trap set by a former fan, due to his desire to experience the adventure and excitement of his former life. He fails to appreciate his wife and family until he almost loses them due to his lack of judgment. Mr. Incredible shows he is able to think quickly on his feet, as well as out-muscle his opponents.

Captain Kirk

James T. Kirk [Star Trek] embodies the phrase, "To boldly go where no man has gone before," leading the Starship Enterprise on many adventures during it's 5-year mission. He also embodies the famous

Stephen Stills song lyric, "Love the one you're with," as he has had many female lovers, both human and alien, during his run as captain. A brilliant tactician, he is able to think of solutions on-the-fly when dealing with a seemingly impossible scenario. Kirk frequently disobeys Starfleet directives. He gets bored and depressed when not on an adventure.

Power Girl

Power Girl [DC Comics] is a great example of how difficult it is to assign a personality type to a fictional character. Her origin has changed several times over the years: from being an Earth-2 Kryptonian version of Supergirl to an Atlantean, and then back to being from Earth-2. It's very difficult to get a fix on her type. We have her listed as a Type 7 partially due to her flamboyant dress and aggressive fighting style. One version of her holds a grudge with Barbara Gordon because of a mission that went awry, resulting in many innocent deaths. She also had a disagreement with Supergirl over the bottled city of Kandor. Power Girl has been a member of many superhero teams over the years.

The Thing

A man on the inside, a monster to the world on the outside, Ben Grimm [Marvel Comics] carries that rocky exterior like a heavy burden. He is at his best when helping out his teammates in the Fantastic Four during a battle. Ben loves to argue with the Human Torch and make fun of Reed Richards. The Thing, at his heart, is just a regular guy from Brooklyn who happens to be a world-class pilot. He fell in love with Alicia Masters, a blind sculptress who loves Ben for who he is, regardless of how he looks. Ben has occasionally reverted back to human form, but always seems to return to his Thing persona to help out his teammates, and because he believes Alicia prefers him that way. He would rather be part of the action, even if he can't stand how he looks.

Sherlock Holmes

The great detective, Sherlock Holmes is able to construct a story with the smallest of details. He is analytical, able to solve any puzzle presented to him, and is an expert at forensics for his time. Holmes counts Dr. Watson as one of his few close friends. Like many 7's, he is energized by new experiences, which for him are new cases to pursue. He also gets bored easily in-between investigations, turning to drugs and tobacco to stimulate his mind, which is common among average 7's we've known in real life. It is easy to think he's a Type 5, but as mentioned throughout this book, traits are not exclusive to one type. In many ways, 7's like Holmes have the ability tap into their direction of integration when they are involved in a project they enthusiastically care about. Unlike 5's, Type 7's like Holmes have the energy and drive to pursue an adventure to the end, unafraid of the challenges and willing to confront dangerous characters, when necessary.

Batman

Born into a wealthy family, Bruce Wayne's life was forever altered by a thug who killed his parents in cold blood on the dark streets of Gotham. While he has exhibited many healthy qualities over the years, such as mentoring youth and teaming up with other heroes, the reason he is listed as an average 7 is because of his unhealthy lifelong obsession with the death of his parents, which led to the creation of the Batman [DC Comics] persona. This persona seems more real than Bruce Wayne. Which is the mask, the super hero or the civilian? The fact this comes up over and over again is a strong indication that Batman, as beloved as he is, has serious issues and is not a fully healthy individual.

Fox Mulder

Fox Mulder [X-Files] is obsessed with UFO's and conspiracy theories. He is a strong-willed FBI agent who stands by his beliefs, despite the agency assigning Scully to debunk him, to the point that Scully eventually is convinced and starts to see things his way. Mulder is driven to find out what happened to his sister. Like other heroic 7's, he is not afraid of facing his enemy. Mulder willingly faces death, bordering on suicidal at times, displaying manic energy. He does not value sleep, and can be brooding at times.

She-Hulk

Fear/Desires: *To live life fully.*

Motivations: *Uses her super powers to battle super villains, and enjoys being She-Hulk even when practicing law.*

Important Life Events: *Given a gamma-irradiated blood transfusion from her unhealthy cousin, Dr. Bruce Banner.*

Reactions Under Stress: *Loves to crack jokes, steal scenes, and act quickly to get things done. Heroic.*

Mental Health Range: *Pretty much lives in the 1 to 3 range, with some average quirks that may slide her down to 4 on occasion.*

The Wing Slider: *Certainly a strong-willed character with a medium 8-wing.*

Instinctive Subtype: *Social.*

Quirks: *Flirtatious, loves being the center of attention, slightly egotistical. These quirks do not make someone unhealthy or average by themselves. It is how someone expresses their quirks that reveals level of healthiness.*

Also Could Be: *Jennifer Walters, before becoming She-Hulk, was briefly characterized as an inhibited person, possibly a Type 1.*

Enneagram Pop is a massive project. It's not something that we just rushed into. It's something that we discussed for decades and then started making lists and jotting names down, but once we sat down and actually went over and "proofed" the characters and their level of healthiness, amazingly enough, we had a low count for healthy Enneagram Type 7s. Initially there were some names on there, but then when we actually put them through the proof, they were just not healthy.

There seems to be a trope in fiction where the writers portray characters as either being healthy or unhealthy, and if they are relaxed they seem average- just normal, everyday people that put on a cape or something. However healthy 7s seem rare in fiction because they are so quirky. We looked at the list Type 7s and said, "Sherlock Holmes: The world's greatest detective, forensics innovator, cultural icon- he has to be healthy. I mean, we know he did drugs and smokes but he's healthy, right?"

Yet when we started to go over his history (we've read most of his cases), he doesn't eat much, he's obsessed, too involved in the work, and doesn't sleep much. That's not healthy; that's not to be emulated by real people. For some reason, this personality is very popular for spin-off characters, like House, agent Mulder, and Batman. None of them are healthy. Initially, we had these characters listed as healthy, and I would say Mulder does show signs of being healthy at the end of the X-Files, but we didn't think he would be good to focus on as an example of a healthy 7 for this book.

Batman might initially appear healthy, right? "He's heroic. He's a DC icon. He dedicates his life to stop criminals." Well, the guy has issues. Major issues. He doesn't know if Bruce Wayne is his main identity or if Batman is. He's a tragic figure, and too obsessed with his parents death. There are times he may have been healthy, but we just didn't feel comfortable focusing on him. For this main feature, we chose She-Hulk.

She-Hulk, unlike Bruce Banner Hulk, actually enjoys being a Hulk. Her name is Jennifer Walters, who is a good defense attorney. Bruce Banner gave her a blood transfusion after she was in an accident. His gamma-irradiated blood made her She-Hulk. Unlike Bruce Banner, who hates his identity, hates himself, and hates turning into the Hulk when he's angry, Jennifer changes at will! She loves it.

7s believe that happiness is out there, and that's why they are into the physical activities and pleasures, whereas 5s are cerebral. Sevens are their opposites (Banner is a 5) and it can be seen like that on the Enneagram diagram, as well.

Jennifer embraces her super strength and being a head-turner. She uses her physical abilities and beauty to do good things: battle monsters, super villains, save the world, join the Avengers, join the Fantastic Four, etc. She feels comfortable in her skin and is much more outgoing as She-Hulk.

When Jennifer Walters was first shown, she was purposely drawn with big round nerdy glasses and dressed up conservatively, like a typical early 80's blue skirt lawyer out in California, but when she's She-Hulk, she's like a model. So, the comic book creators wanted to show that the original Jennifer Walters was inhibited and shy. She likes to stay as She-Hulk, and even practices law currently as She-Hulk. She doesn't have a need to go back to being human. Would you?

The reason why She-Hulk is on the high-spectrum of healthiness is because she's free-spirited, spontaneous, cheerful, outgoing, adventurous, energetic, stimulated, responsive, quick, resilient, positive, grateful, truly free, content, ecstatic, accomplished, versatile, entertaining, self-confident. Yes, that's a bunch of adjectives! And they all describe Sevens. On the rare appearances where She-Hulk and Hulk teamed up back in the 80s, when they were side-by-side, you could really see how Jennifer Walters is light-years more healthy than Bruce Banner and the Hulk.

One thing about 7s, even healthy 7s, is that they're still egotistical. They still have that aspect where they have to be the center of attention. They feed off of it. That's how they get their energy. They can't be lonely. Something always has to be happening. They tap into that unlimited energy that they have. There's nothing wrong with that at all because actions make the world go 'round, not inaction or idle philosophies.

It does show you that, even at the healthy ends of the spectrum, the quirks of the 7 just don't go away. The She-Hulk is 100% entertaining, and a scene-stealer in the comics. She cracks jokes, and is shown as a beautiful green-skinned Amazon with a perfect body and pretty face. She's flirtatious, and we're not going to penalize a woman for being flirtatious on the healthy scale. It just doesn't make sense to do that, especially since she's a 7 and they enjoy attention or recognition.

It's easy to underestimate or judge the She-Hulk if you don't know the character, thinking that she's all brawn and beauty, and no brains, but she is a very intelligent and powerful attorney. Early on in her career, she used to rush into things, but she's been able to step back a little bit in the modern era. She still has that action aspect that all 7's have.

The bottom line is that She-Hulk is amazingly popular, even though she's always been reduced to a second string character. There's probably too much cheesecake involved with her. Artists put her in a bikini on the covers. John Byrne, the writer and artist who took her over at one point, had her break the fourth wall, and I don't think she's ever recovered from that to be treated as a serious character. Marvel depicts her to be a comedy character. That fits in the personality of the 7. The 7 is the practical joker, but we feel that she, as a character, never reached her potential, and ultimately it's a bit sexist for Marvel to treat her as lesser Hulk.

That being said, she is a great example of what a healthy 7 can be. She's not self-destructive, rude, and she's not addicted to anything harmful. Her only "flaw" is that she enjoys being a superhero, but in the context of comic books, that's fine. She enjoys being a woman that can lift 100's of tons. That's not a drawback.

When you compare her mental stability to, say, Ben Grimm, (she has worked side-by-side with The Thing, another 7) you can see that she's much more happy, and enjoys life. She was never depressed or suicidal in the comics, like Ben Grimm was, and she does not have the mommy/daddy issues that Bruce Wayne has. So, that's why She-Hulk is the example of the healthy 7: she focuses her energy on positive action.

What we've learned:
- Sevens are so intense, funny, or action-oriented that they are always in the center of attention.
- Healthy Sevens are a force to be reckoned with; without self-destructive tendencies, they can achieve greatness and true happiness.

- Healthy Sevens focus their energy and get things done; unhealthy and average Sevens have racing thoughts and lack the commitment to finish projects or goals.
- Even Healthy types retain personality quirks. The implication is that even the most enlightened or self-actualized being still wears a mask. The key is that they know it is a mask.

Other Healthy 7's
Colt Seavers

Colt Seavers is a Hollywood stuntman by day, and a bounty hunter by night to pay the bills. He is a great example of a Type 7 who has focused on developing one set of skills (stunt work), and applying those same skills to another trade (bounty hunting). Colt is relatively drama free, and audiences got bored with the villain of the week storylines after five seasons. Like other sevens, he plays the role of mentor and team leader well.

Part Eight
Type 8

Hulk

Fear/Desires: Does not trust anyone.

Motivations: Lashes out in rage and anger against those he perceives to be out to get him.

Important Life Events: Dr. Banner blasted with Gamma Radiation while saving Rick Jones. Hunted and hounded by the military, led by General Ross. Assumed Mr. Fixit Las Vegas persona at one time. Was exiled to a distant planet where he became a leader.

Reactions Under Stress: Like an unstoppable force of nature, the Hulk gets stronger the angrier he gets. He is impossible to reason with when he is angry.

Mental Health Range: He is the epitome of the ugly side of Enneagram Type 8, existing in the unhealthy levels of 7 through 9, and occasionally shows an average side in the 5-6 range when he is the Grey Hulk.

The Wing Slider: A straight 8.

Instinctive Subtype: The Hulk wants to survive. Self-preservation is his subtype.

Quirks: Very similar to Godzilla, in terms of fictional 8's who are forces of nature embodied in a character. Like most 8's that want to control their world, Hulk is very single-minded.

Also Could Be: N/A. Although it is strange that Dr. Banner, a Type 5, becomes an unhealthy Type 8 in what should be the healthy direction of integration, this does not prove the Hulk is another Enneagram personality type, like a Type 7 in Dr. Banner's direction of disintegration. Perhaps the answer is that the Hulk is the core type, who disintegrates into five.

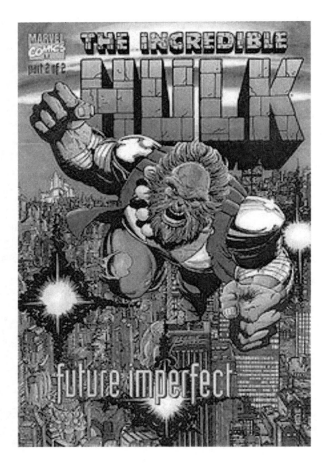

There's only one iconic Marvel super hero that is truly inhuman, monstrous, barbarous, omnipotent, vindictive, anti-social, vengeful, violent, and brutal. He is the Hulk- an unstoppable force fueled by his rage and anger.

He doesn't trust anyone, and is a primal animal. This is based on his instincts to survive, and further developed by the humans, military, and other super-powered beings that always pick on him, and get him even more angry. Then he becomes even more destructive.

The Hulk is the ultimate 8 of the Marvel Universe, if not all of comicdom. His personality is a sick, twisted mirror of Dr. Bruce Banner, who is an Enneagram Type 5. Creators Stan Lee and Jack Kirby used Dr. Jekyll and Mr. Hyde as an inspiration.

Healthy 5's integrate into healthy 8's, but when Lee and Kirby created the Hulk, they unknowingly reversed the system. So, the unhealthy Banner disintegrates to a irrational 8. The Enneagram system is set up for an unhealthy 5 to fall to an unhealthy 7. Of course, if we wanted a No-Prize to defend that problem, Lee and Kirby may have set up the dual identity for the Hulk to be the core personality who falls to Banner, an unhealthy 5.

There are a few different archetypes for 8. For example, an 8 can be your mean mother-in-law, or a corrupt CEO, or a cruel dictator. There is also a type of 8, like the Hulk or Godzilla. These types of 8's are forces of nature, seemingly Invincible. They will not surrender. They would rather destroy the entire world than to give up.

The angrier the Hulk gets, the stronger he becomes. His power level is unlimited because of this ability. When the Marvel heroes decided that the Hulk was too dangerous to stay on Earth, he was exiled into space. He swore vengeance. However, with no way back, he found a new life for himself on another planet (Planet Hulk storyline). It was a planet where it was survival of the fittest, and, well, the Hulk is the most fit. He adapted well in that planet and was respected, as he had no rules or morality in a dog-eat-dog world where everyone had super powers. He became their king, found a wife, and she became pregnant. For the first time in his life, the Hulk was happy and was worshipped. He was an inspirational leader and was finally content in his role.

And then the planet blew up. He lost everything he cared for, including his wife, and, he believed, his unborn child. He blamed the heroes for this, because that's what the evidence showed. Swearing vengeance, he went back to Earth and he took out every single hero he held responsible, and anyone that dared cross his path (World War Hulk storyline.)

Maybe you're thinking, "Okay, Professor X can shut his mind down, or Dr. Strange can send him to another dimension, or Thor may knock him out with a lightning bolt from the heavens," but not this time. The Hulk was so full of anger and vengeance, that he skinned Wolverine, blocked Professor X's mental attacks, took out Iron Man, and all the other teams and heroes, right in New York, too. His mind was full of inner chaos, and he had no regrets. He had a single-minded focus to just destroy. Destroy. Destroy.

The Hulk doesn't need to speak. Over the many, many decades in his publishing history, there are times when he just growls: "Grrrr!" Other times, he'll speak without verbs or complete sentences, or the noun structure is messed up: "Hulk smash!" We recall a situation when one of our co-workers, a Type 8, had an email correspondence with another 8: two 8's communicating with each other. The other 8, from the other company, responded back with "???", and the 8 that we knew went totally crazy, because he totally understood the frustration and confusion on the other 8's part. He went to customer service and started demanding that the problem be fixed. We find it humorous because 8's don't need to speak. A mere question mark, grunt, or grimace shall suffice. The Hulk is a great symbol of that.

Bruce Banner was physically abused as a child. His father killed his mother. His father also had radiation in his genes. Thus, Banner was destined to become the Hulk and release that inner torment as a physical manifestation. In truth, he just wants to be loved, but he pushes everyone away. So, it's impossible to love him.

The Hulk has multiple personalities, but all can be covered by the Type Eight: from being rebellious, to infantile, to a genius, to monstrous, or to a clever strategist. Occasionally the Hulk assumes a Mr. Fixit persona, which was a Las Vegas bodyguard/gambler type who enjoys being a seedy outlaw, and relished in hedonism.

It should be noted that the Hulk is not a hero or villain, per se; he is an anti-hero, one of the earliest anti-heroes in comic books. If you just leave him alone, he won't smash you. And he smashes more villains than heroes.

Anyway, it should be noted that even when Bruce Banner's mind does take control of the Hulk, the Hulk is still, at his core being, an 8, not a 5. So, even with all that power, the Hulk's personality subdues Banner's Type 5 personality. This was shown many times in the comic books, over the years. Inside the head and mind of Banner and the Hulk, they have a duel, and the Hulk is usually able to build a wall around the Banner persona.

The Hulk is the ultimate 8 in all of comics. Keep a lookout for other characters in fiction that are like the Hulk. It's the primal force Type 8: the irrational, unstoppable force.

What we've learned:
- Eights are run by instincts, as well as physical and emotional needs, more than the other types, and will act to fulfill them.
- Eights have many different subtype roles that may not seem related, but generally share the core traits of not relying on others and being without sensitivity.
- Eights may seem like Fours (independent and outlaws) but are not as "deep". Another major difference is that a Four can be content with finding a soulmate, while an Eight needs to be in charge of something (usually the environment).
- Eights needs to feel in control of their lives, and you'd better steer clear if they feel helpless.
- Eights are masters of non-verbal communication.
- An unhealthy Eight is perhaps the most destructive of all the types.
- Eights naturally like to be in charge, and if they are not in that role, they will fight (or complain).
- Anger, rage, hostility, persecution, unhappiness, expecting a tough life: these are reasons why Eights seem mean.
- An Eight's mind may seem chaotic, primal, and undisciplined, but it's perfectly normal to them. They are motivated by their passions.

Other Unhealthy 8's

Magneto

Erik Lensherr, a.k.a. Magneto [Marvel Comics], originally started as a "by any means necessary" Malcolm X clone, juxtaposed to Professor X and his peaceful resistance stance. Over the years, he became more of an anti-hero, eventually renewing his friendship with Professor X and even taking over as Headmaster of Mutant High. At his worst, he is a psychopathic murderer who believes he is superior to humanity, and he is willing to kill fellow mutants who disagree with his agenda.

Skeletor

Skeletor [Masters of the Universe] is determined to take over Castle Grayskull in the Filmation cartoon, *Masters of the Universe*, from the 1980's. He surrounds himself with powerful and loyal henchmen, such as Merman, Tri-Klops, and Beastman. Skeletor uses magic and technology in executing his evil plans. He is always cooking up a scheme, and always seems to have an escape plan handy when things go awry.

Megatron

Leader of the evil Decepticons, Megatron [Transformers] is the sworn enemy of Optimus Prime. He enjoys killing Autobots. Like Skeletor, he surrounds himself with lackeys who he can boss around. Megatron craves power and total control. He chooses destructive means to meet his goals.

Godzilla

Like the Hulk, Godzilla [Toho] is a Type 8 who is akin to a force of nature. Armies cannot stand against him. A child of the atomic bomb, Godzilla is a reflection of the destructive force of nuclear weapons. At times, Godzilla has also been a defender of Japan against other nuclear-powered monsters, as well as aliens and giant robots. In these instances, he is treated as misunderstood by society, and reverentially by those he has saved from destruction.

Anti-Monitor

If a healthy Type 9 like the Monitor has an exact antithesis, it would be the Anti-Monitor [DC Comics]. Born on the planet Qward in the anti-matter universe as the result of a scientific experiment by Krona to see the birth of the universe, the Anti-Monitor and Monitor balanced each other out for millions of years. The Anti-Monitor, after conquering his universe, eventually found a method to destroy the multiverse using anti-matter, absorbing the energy from each universe as he went. He attempted to go back to the beginning of time in order to stop the creation of the multiverse, and was thwarted by powerful magical beings like the Spectre. Refusing to die, the Anti-Matter came back one last time to destroy the sole remaining universe, and was thwarted by the original Superman and Superboy from Earth-Prime. The Anti-Monitor was completely maniacal, power-hungry, and focused on his goals: to defeat his counterpart, destroy the multiverse, and rule the one remaining anti-matter universe.

Guy Gardner

Fear/Desires: To be admired/respected by other super heroes.

Motivations: Antagonizes and confronts others in order to assert his control over the group he's in.

Important Life Events: Became friends with Hal Jordan. Trapped in the Phantom Zone, where his brain was damaged. Founding member of Justice League International.

Reactions Under Stress: Confrontational. Will sacrifice himself to get the job done.

Mental Health Range: Lives in the 5 to 8 range.

The Wing Slider: Has a 7-wing.

Instinctive Subtype: Social.

Quirks: Can be mean, pushy, and over-the-top. Lives to draw reactions from others.

Also Could Be: 7's, 3's, and 4's may get in your face, but for different reasons than a Type 8.

Guy Gardner is a controversial Green Lantern who is known for being obnoxious, cocky, arrogant, hard-headed, confrontational, and immature. Guy works on sheer willpower and thinks he's right all the time. We've worked professionally with people who exhibit the different Enneagram Types, and lived with family members, and we can vouch that Type Eights can completely disrupt a group and cause severe fights in a confrontational manner. Sure, Type Sevens, Threes, and Fours can get in your face, but the motives and styles are different. An Average Eight wants to control his or her environment, desires to be admired or needed, has a huge ego, and demonstrates a willingness to draw out reactions and emotions from people. Average Eights love to antagonize; it makes them feel alive.

Guy Gardner is such an over the top fictional character that some readers in the comic book letter pages have questioned if anyone actually acts like that in real life. Well, if they kept their eyes and ears open they should have noticed a mean boss, pushy relative, spoiled brat, or schoolyard bully who acted in the same way.

Gardner is not just a goofball (like some crazy Sixes or Sevens). He works on the power of his will and never backs down from a challenge. He works on instincts and passion. He is very defensive about his skills and ego. In his prime, he didn't get along with the other characters in the DC Universe. He has mellowed in recent years, but still is outspoken and tough.

Guy's negative personality traits are said to be the result of brain damage, although he was always aggressive, and even was arrested for stealing cars as a juvenile. Trying to justify his behavior due to brain damage is funny because with Average Eights it seems like that is the only explanation for their socially inappropriate and offensive behavior (think of all the offensive things another fictional Eight- Archie Bunker of "All in the Family"- says about groups of people, or the real-life Archie, Rush Limbaugh). Suffice to say, Average Eights don't need brain damage to be mean. (Please note: not all Average Eights are mean, but they do speak their minds, which may hurt your feelings, especially if you didn't ask for their input. They keep anger management, marriage, and sexual harassment counselors in business)

The 1980s version of Guy Gardner in Justice League International was modeled after the testosterone macho world of Ronald Reagan, Rambo, and Arnold Schwarzenegger. Guy is an "ask questions later" - or never- action hero. His prankish behavior and scatterbrained schemes with the Justice League International showed that he has a Seven wing.

Gardner has been envious of Hal Jordan, the so-called greatest Green Lantern, and had tried to outshine and compete with Hal on every matter. Guy was designated as a replacement for Hal, and Guy believes he is the chosen one, not Hal. Hal is a Type Six, who are usually targets for Eights (see J. Jonah Jameson vs Peter Parker, Perry White vs Clark Kent). When stripped of the ring, Guy stole Sinestro's yellow ring. Guy constantly tried to prove himself as being worthy.

Eights have been called "The Boss", "The Leader", or "The Challenger" by other authors; well Gardner was frustrated that he was not given that role. So an Eight who is not a respected (or feared) authority figure will complain, disrupt, and rebel against whoever is in charge. This is the path of becoming an outlaw or outcast.

So what's so good about Guy Gardner? Why isn't he Unhealthy? Well, he's an anti-hero in comics. An anti-hero is a hero that doesn't follow the traditional code of honor and acts like a cad. So although he's mean, breaks the rules, and will kill, he believes in justice. He is an intergalactic lawman. He will make sacrifices, does his job well, is not *always* manic, and has a hidden romantic side. Over the years, he has calmed down and shown responsibility. Guy has grown and evolved, and is no longer a one-dimensional Eight as he was depicted in the 1980s.

What we've learned:
- Eights are very aggressive, tough, rough, crude, and full of energy.
- Eights feel alive by fighting, challenging, and arguing with others. Unfortunately, this can come off as being juvenile, immature, or disrespectful.
- Due to their outspokenness and lack of subtlety, Some Eights are prone to be politically incorrect, and may have strong views on gender, race, or politics.
- Average Eights can be action-oriented leaders or authority figures, which are their natural dispositions.
- Eights are highly competitive and prone to jealousy and envy. Unlike some other types that just think about making changes, Eights will do what it takes to be the best.
- An average 8w7 is going to be a handful for anyone.

- Eights and Sixes have "heat".

Other Average 8's
J. Jonah Jameson

Editor-in-Chief of the Daily Bugle, J. Jonah Jameson [Marvel Comics] personifies the wheeling-dealing Type 8 who is clearly in charge: demanding, pushy, and bending others to his will. His conflict with Peter Parker and Spider Man is a classic example of 6 versus 8 conflict. At the end of the day, J.J.J. just wants to sell newspapers and make a profit. Spider Man is a perfect recurring foil for the front page headlines. He under-pays Parker because he views him as a kid and his association with Spider Man; older 8's are willing to treat peers with more respect, and dish out the dough when needed.

Nerys Kira

Raised in a refugee camp during the Cardassian occupation, Nerys Kira [Star Trek: DS9] grew up without her mother and in the midst of war. She became part of the resistance movement, and eventually ended up on the Deep Space Nine space station as a Bajoran militia officer. Kira was instrumental in organizing the resistance against the Dominion. She played hard-to-get with Odo until the end of the series. Kira butted heads with Commander Sisko and initially disagreed with Federation involvement in Bajor, but became a trusted 2nd-in-command and a Starfleet Officer. She was frequently in life-or-death situations, and prone to being possessed.

Princess Leia

Leader of the Rebellion against the Empire, Princess Leia Organa [Star Wars] works to subvert the system. She plays hot and cold with Han Solo during the Original Trilogy, expressing her love for him only when it was too late. Stubborn. A diplomat by trade, she is skilled at getting along with alien races like the Ewoks. She uses her regal status to get things done. Very street smart, she is not afraid to bluff a dictator or crime lord.

Quark

Owner of a bar/gambling hall aboard Starbase Deep Space Nine, Quark [Star Trek: DS9] is known for dealing in black market products and illegal events. He constantly clashes with Security Officer Odo, and loves to bend the rules in his favor. Quark embraces capitalism, which is a big part of Ferengi culture. Like average 8's we know in real life, he has a soft side for those in need under his gruff exterior.

Teela

Daughter of the Sorceress and raised by Man-at-Arms, Teela [Masters of the Universe] is the head of the palace guards, and is charged with protecting Prince Adam of Eternia from harm. She is very confident, and frequently chides Prince Adam for being lazy. She is also known to lose her temper and then make poor decisions. Disconnected from both biological parents during childhood, Teela did not learn that the Sorceress was her mother until adulthood.

Perry White

Before J.J.J., there was Perry White [DC Comics]. He is one of the original comic book characterizations of a newspaper Editor-in-chief, and a bit more level-headed than his Marvel Comics counterpart. White ran the Daily Planet for many years. He views Superman as a hero, and treats him fairly in the headlines. His famous catchphrase is, "Great Caesar's Ghost!" Jimmy Olson, Lois Lane, and Clark Kent are all loyal to him, to a certain extent.

Frank Barone

Frank is the curmudgeonly old patriarch of the Barone family who represents people from his generation who have difficulty saying things like, "I love you." He is like an apolitical Archie Bunker, complete with his favorite chair and his drinking buddies that he hangs out with at the lodge. Unlike Archie, he is a more of a funny Type 8, like a J. Jonah Jameson. His catch-phrase is, "Holy crap!" Frank enjoys bossing his wife around and needling her when she's wrong about something. He loves to make fun of Ray and Robert when they're going through a struggle. Like most typical 8's, when he finally does reveal his true emotions, he's very shy about it. He is afraid of his true self being exposed, so he just chooses to show the crazy, hard exterior. He is pretty much impossible to live with, as highlighted in the one episode where Marie and Frank tried to move into a condo community and were kicked out, partly because Frank was trying to run over security guards with his golf cart, as well as stealing food from the community fridge.

Yoda

Fear/Desires: To bring balance to the Force.

Motivations: Works to prevent the return of the Sith.

Important Life Events: Allows Obi-Wan to train Anakin after the death of Qui-Gon. Goes into exile after being defeated by the Emperor. After placing his faith in the Force, his faith was rewarded with the arrival of Anakin's son on Dagobah.

Reactions Under Stress: Willing to fight, if necessary.

Mental Health Range: Yoda is a wizened old Type 8 who has left behind some of the competitive fire that comes with youth. He is a battle-hardened individual who lives in the 1 to 3 range of mental health during the movies.

The Wing Slider: A strong 9-wing.

Instinctive Subtype: Self-Preservation.

Quirks: Assertive opinions, with no regrets (with one major exception, thanks to George Lucas).

Also Could Be: Since he is a mentor, many online argue that he is a Type 1.

We were going to stay away from Star Wars characters, only because we don't think creator George Lucas was consistent with some of the characterizations and how he was setting up his universe using the Hero's Journey formula. For example, there's way too many mentors in Star Wars, and Lucas has borrowed elements from other sources, in our opinion (such as Jack Kirby's New Gods).

In the Hero's Journey template, which thousands of writers have used over the years, the mentor is supposed to be the wise teacher who doesn't really engage in action, which is like a Type 1, the spiritual teacher. Of course, you can have other types be a mentor, but they are generally supposed to be theoretical in nature. Therefore some fans online don't see Yoda as an 8.

First of all, one reason people don't see it is because Yoda's not the typical 8 physically, like the Hulk, Godzilla, or the Anti-Monitor; he's a little muppet. Lucas was playing a little trick on us about Yoda's deceptive physical appearance. When Yoda first made his appearance, in The Empire Strikes Back, we were as much in the dark as Luke Skywalker was. We didn't know any of the history of Yoda; we just saw a little Kermit the Frog in the swamp, and we were laughing. Right away, when you compare that version of Yoda, his first appearance in Episode 5, to the other movies, and you can see that the characterization is a bit off.

In other words, first impressions last forever. The first impression of Yoda is him being a little practical joker with no powers. Then, of course, we see that he's just tricking Luke and testing him, but first impressions last a lifetime. There are a few reasons why he's not an obvious 8 and a few reasons why people may challenge it, but here goes.

Taken in the whole, all the movies, he is very assertive with his opinions, he is very strong-willed, and he's the boss of all the Jedi. Being the leader should be a little sign right there, at least a starting point for his candidacy for being an 8. From there we can see that he's not a pushover leader. He may take your suggestions at heart and he may think about them, but he's going to make his own decision and have no regrets about it, unless he's exiled to a planet until he dies, but that's besides the point there. Yoda balances logic with instincts and foresight. Compare and contrast Yoda with Spock (Type 1), who just uses rational thought and no heart.

The actual textbook for the Enneagram, *Personality Types* by Don Richard Riso and Russ Hudson, has a phrase for healthy 8's. It says,

"Have a vision." Yeah, that's pretty funny, because throughout the Star Wars movies, Yoda can see future timelines and spirits. So, he definitely has vision- taking it both figuratively and literally.

Metaphorically speaking, Yoda wanted a world, a universe that has balance in the Force, but skewed toward Jedi, of course. He hated the Sith and did not want them to take over at all. A Type 1 or Type 9 character would make compromises or follow a strict 50/50 balance.

Yoda was one not to shy from tough decisions. Also, You see him as a master war strategist in the new trilogy. Ultimately, when he dies in Return of the Jedi, he's very inspiring to Luke, and to the viewers as well. He's very a spiritual 8, which is the greatest sign of healthiness. He's been around for 100's and 100's of years. One reason why some people may not see him as an 8 is that he's battle-hardened. In his old age, he becomes gentle and selfless.

Eights have such a dominant personality, that it is hard to forget or ignore them. The average Eights are just so competitive and business-like that the compassion just gets thrown out. Yet toward the end, Yoda really has compassion. Even early on, in the new trilogies, he is healthy. Come on, the guy has already been in business for 100's of years- he's an enlightened individual, the head of a pseudo-religious warrior clan. The way he's shown, he's like the Dalai Lama on steroids.

Yoda is someone you don't want to cross. If you cross a 1, they may sue you. If you cross a 2, you will get hit with a guilt trip. Cross an 8, and you can be in serious trouble. He's no nonsense and can fight on his own. He has superpowers and shows them as a mental and physical warrior, but his spiritual side is the one that really shines.

Interestingly enough, Yoda is an 8 who has retired and is "done", which is rare for an 8 but is a testament of George Lucas' problem with characterization more than Yoda. When we first see Yoda on Dagobah, he's in exile, has no friends, is living in a hut, and he's completely done with the war against the Sith. So, Lucas painted himself in a corner. When he wrote the new trilogies, Episodes I to III, he had to show why Yoda was there. To us, it's kind of a stretch to have Yoda give up. An

Eight would continue to plan. There may be some expanded universe novel where Yoda is working behind the scenes and training a whole bunch of Jedis before Luke, setting up a whole war on the other side of the galaxy. Or maybe not, but this profile is not about the expanded universe. In this case, the Yoda profile is about the original and prequel trilogies that we all saw.

Now, the only defense we can come up with is that Yoda was an enlightened individual, like the Dalai Lama, or like a Buddha, where he wanted to live out the rest of his life and meditate on a swamp planet, all by himself. He just lost so much and there was no possible way to defeat the Sith with what was known at the time. Also, Anakin betrayed the Jedi and he didn't see it. He said, "Done I am. Stay here I will. The Force will do something that is destined." Sure enough, Anakin Skywalker's son shows up on that planet. That's when Yoda knows that maybe this is his last chance to help bring balance to the Force.

What we've learned:
- A healthy Eight may be the best leader.
- Eights are master strategists and capable of seeing the motives of different factions.
- Compassion is the key trait which separates Healthy Eights from Average and Unhealthy Eights.
- Eights are visionaries.
- Because most writers do not use the Enneagram, there may be inconsistencies in characterization.
- Do not accept one person's opinion about Enneagram types from an internet message board: get to the root of the Type using the methods we have described here.

Other Healthy 8's
Battle-Cat
Like the Hulk and Godzilla, Battle-Cat [Masters of the Universe] exemplifies the force of nature aspect of Enneagram Type 8 and is a beast. Unlike his unhealthy counterparts, Battle-Cat displays the healthy attributes of his type. He is courageous and selfless in battle, and is protective of his master, He-Man. Battle-Cat shares another thing in common with the Hulk: his personality type is separate and distinct from his alter ego, Cringer, who is a phobic Type 6.

Lt. Worf
Adopted by a human family, Worf [Star Trek: TNG] has strong emotional ties to his Klingon heritage. He is loyal to his ancestors and traditions, despite not being fully accepted by fellow Klingons. Worf is a courageous security officer. He is stubborn at times, but is able to accept advice even if he initially disagrees. Worf exhibits patience and control, and expresses himself when necessary. He killed the man who murdered his son's mother in a deathmatch, per Klingon tradition.

Part Nine
Type 9

Anakin Skywalker

Fear/Desires: Fears the loss of loved ones.

Motivations: Attempts to bring order to the galaxy in an attempt to assuage his guilt and feelings of loss.

Important Life Events: Winning a Pod-race on Tatooine that leads to his freedom. Failing to save his mother. Marrying Padme. Turning to the Dark Side, becoming Emperor Palpatine's servant. Being encased in a mechanical body after his defeat at the hands of Obi-Wan Kenobi. Discovering his son and daughter were still alive. Defeating the Emperor in order to save his son.

Reactions Under Stress: Violent. Sullen. Lashes out thoughtlessly, vengefully, at the object of his scorn. Homicidal.

Mental Health Range: Anakin Skywalker travels through all 9 levels of health in the six Star Wars: at times heroic, other times murderous. The unhealthy Darth Vader persona exists in the 7 to 9 health range.

The Wing Slider: Given his passionate, headstrong side as revealed in the prequels, Anakin must have a strong 8-wing.

Instinctive Subtype: Sexual.

Quirks: Falling to temptation is a trait amongst unhealthy nines, as is their ability to appear good, making you think they will turn around before falling into further darkness.

Also Could Be: The Personality Type book by Riso and Hudson, as well as many online forums, suggest Darth Vader is actually an 8 with a strong 9 wing.

Those new to the Enneagram may link up a villain like Darth Vader to various dictators in real life such as Hitler, or famous comic book villains like Doctor Doom or Lex Luthor, but even as kids, when we were first exposed to Star Wars, Vader seemed different. For such a grand villain, in the original trilogy, Vader seems dead on the inside. He's very subservient to the Emperor. Most famous villains are not subservient. There was a conflict going on inside of Darth Vader, and he redeemed himself at the end.

Years later, the new trilogy explored his childhood, growth emotionally, and his fall. It turns out that Anakin Skywalker/Darth Vader is a textbook Enneagram Type 9. His story should be a warning and a lesson to other Type 9's.

As a child, he was easy-going, outgoing, friendly, gentle, steady, and optimistic- a good kid. He and his mother were slaves, and young Ani was brought up in a harsh life without a father to influence him. However, one would be hard-pressed to predict that he would become a stone-cold murderer and dictator of so many different planetary systems and galaxies in the Star Wars Universe.

He was attached to his mother. We know many 9s that are attached to their mothers- big time. The male Nines we have interviewed consider their mothers to be a sacred part of their lives, and they have martyred their parent. Even the most innocuous joke or objective question could be misconstrued by a 9 regarding his mother, or child, or spouse. Accordingly, these male Nines tend to judge all other women based on their mom. To non-Nines, it's weird.

Anakin had to leave his mother. That was to be the event that changed his smile to a frown, although not immediately. His age of innocence was over, however. He was attached to her, and never got over it.

When we were next introduced to Anakin Skywalker, in Episode 2, he is no longer that even-keeled kid. He doesn't listen anymore, and longs to rescue his mother. It could be argued that he was always independently-minded, even as a kid, the way he built his robot C-3PO and strove to participate in the Pod Race. He was out-going to strangers, but when we see him as a teenager, there's much anger in him, and frustration. He lives in this fantasy world where he can leave the Jedi Order, free his mom, and fall in love with a Princess or Queen, which goes against the code. Nines are prone to daydreaming and fantasizing about changing their environment. The grass is greener on the other side of the fence.

So, he let his inner passions get the best of him. Nines don't like to express emotions outwardly. Nines are peacemakers to the extent where they will pretend to be polite to avoid confrontation. (Some Nines are aware of the acting, while others have subconsciously convinced themselves that they truly are not offended or angry.) They'd rather sit it out and not start a fight by expressing their opinions. They really have to be pushed to explode, after that anger builds up. For Anakin, not seeing his mom, her being a slave someplace for ten years, and him not being allowed his one crush in life, Padme, was enough for him to embrace the anger in himself.

Nines can relate to that. Male Nines have a weakness for women. When we interviewed the various types over the years, male Nines and male Fours easily fall in love quickly and hard. Thus they are prone to having their hearts broken or becoming frustrated. They engage in romantic fantasies, acting out, and secretive thrill-seeking. Whereas the Four can move on to another crush, the Nine tends to become obsessed and even stalk their "one true love", who subconsciously reminds them of their mothers.

With each scene, you can tell Anakin is slowly regressing to the unhealthy levels. He's very combative and belligerent with his master, Obi-Wan Kenobi. Like many 9s in fiction and in reality, they show sparks of goodness inside them. For a moment they listen, such as when Anakin tells Obi-Wan that he's like a father to him. They give you that hope that they will turn it around, because they're smart and nod their heads, indicating that they are absorbing your words. You know they're good kids on the inside, and you know they're sensitive. Many other types don't have that sensitivity.

A few types are prone to being sensitive or "humanistic", and 9's are part of that group. Twos, Fours, Sixes, and Nines are sensitive types; meaning, by default, they're prone to caring about what you feel. They'll listen to try to better themselves or not to hurt anyone.

Eventually, Anakin no longer becomes compliant to his training, the code, or his master. He becomes selfish, and he's obsessed. Eventually, he becomes tempted. Of all the types, 9's are the most prone to be tempted, although a Two is a close second due to peer pressure.

Doc Gooden, a famous and tragic 9, is a great example of that. He had a bad day, as a baseball pitcher. The media was reporting about his performance, which was not as good as his phenomenal first season (although still great) and everything fell apart when a cousin of his invited him to a party and put cocaine on the table. The peer pressure got the best of Doc, and he was trying to escape his stress. He snorted the coke. Now, if he could take back one day in his life, it would be that day.

The point is that, under stress, 9's will give in, even though they know better. They will sit there and they will stare at you and they will tell you, "Yes, of course it's wrong to do drugs! Of course it's wrong to over-eat! Of course it's wrong to cheat on your spouse! Of course it's wrong to [insert your favorite vice]," because that's what 9's are the master of: secret lives and internal monologues.

Of course they know better. Many are religious. Anakin Skywalker was training to be a Jedi Knight. In fact, his blood count showed that he had the best potential of any Jedis in training. But he blew it.

Emperor Palpatine, before he was emperor, as Chancellor, got into Anakin's head. He capitalized on Anakin's desires. He could stroke a 9's ego, because they feel, like Anakin felt, under-appreciated. Anyway, Palpatine manipulated him. Anakin's first breaking point came when his mother was killed by Tusken Raiders- sand people. Anakin killed them all out of an act of vengeance, and he killed the women, children, and probably the two little dogs, too.

And then he got married! So, we think, "Alright. Maybe he still has a chance. Maybe he'll not go further down and disintegrate. He's married now! What can go wrong?"

Well, he had dreams that his wife, Padme, was going to do die during childbirth. Thus, he decided he would do anything necessary to prevent that. Then Palpatine got into his head totally, and Anakin sold out. Literally. He just gave his soul up.

Things didn't go right, he totally turned evil, was implicit in the murder of Mace Windu, killed innocent kids that were trained to be Jedis ... the list is numerous of all the sins Anakin committed in that short time, and then he finally battled and lost the duel with his old master, Obi-Wan Kenobi. His body was destroyed: his legs, his hands, his face. Palpatine then saved him and rebuilt him as a half-man, half machine.

Palpatine lied to him, again. He told him that he was responsible for the death of Padme, even though she died during childbirth because she was depressed. He conveniently left that little detail out for the man that is now known as Darth Vader.

As far as Vader's career goes, he turned all his emotions off and just reveled in being desolate and numb- wasted, an empty shell of his former self. He was like that in Episode 4 and 5. And then, in Episode 6, we saw that spark again a little bit, because his son, Luke Skywaker, believed in him. Skywalker is also a 9. He's in his father's image, but he was never fully tempted like Vader was, and he always did the right thing. That inspired him, as it should inspire all Nines.

Then, finally, Luke pushed Vader all the way to finally turn good and against the Emperor, who had just revealed that he also used Vader, and viewed him as a tool. He wanted Luke to be at his side, instead of Vader. Then, yes, Vader redeemed himself at the end, dying in Luke's arms:

Luke: I'll not leave you here, I've got to save you.
Anakin: You already... have, Luke. You were right. You were right about me. Tell your sister... you were right.

Throughout the movie, Luke keeps saying, "There is good in you. I won't join you. I won't join the Emperor. Come with me." And, it turns out he was right- there was good in him. The Force forgave Anakin, and so did Obi-Wan, because Anakin is a ghost, along with Obi-Wan and Yoda, at the end of Return of Jedi.

For Anakin, we have the rise, fall, and redemption. He's a very complex character. Never underestimate a 9: they may seem laid back and inexpressive at times, but there's a lot going on in there, and they only share that with their very close friends or family members.

Suffice to say, in all of fiction, love or hate him, George Lucas did show all the levels of development of Enneagram Type 9 with the journey of Anakin Skywalker to Darth Vader.

What we've learned:
- Nines are prone to temptation.
- Nines will not express their needs openly, until it's too late.
- Male Nines transfer their excessive love and attachment of their mother to other women they encounter later in life.
- Nines are "nice" and sensitive, like Twos, Fours, and Sixes.
- Nines have active imaginations, fantasies, and dreams, and can be lost in them.
- Nines rank happiness (internal mental balance and family) as a top goal in their lives.
- Nines can easily give in to peer pressure and temptation,

depending on their stress levels and emotional needs.
- Unhealthy Nines are infamous for their tragic stories due to their high potential when younger.

Other Unhealthy 9's
Cigarette Smoking Man
Destroyer of evidence to protect a secret government conspiracy, the Cigarette Smoking Man [X-Files] is also the secret assassin who killed JFK and MLK Jr. He refuses to reveal the truth to Mulder and Scully until the bitter end, which is reminiscent of Darth Vader. He is eerily calm and passive in the face of death.

Lana Lang (Smallville)
Fear/Desires: To dream.
Motivations: Stays quiet and keeps her feelings to herself, unless she's pushed, in which case she over-expresses herself.
Important Life Events: On-again, off-again relationship with Clark. Moves to Metropolis. Married, then divorced Lex. Became super-powered. Defused kryptonite bomb and was unable to be near Clark as a result.
Reactions Under Stress: Withdraws. Indecisive.
Mental Health Range: Lives in the 4 to 7 range.
The Wing Slider: No wing.
Instinctive Subtype: Self-Preservation.
Quirks: Has problems expressing her emotions.
Also Could Be: Is into romance and relationships, but unlike, say, an average 4, is out of touch with her instincts.

Lana Lang from the Smallville TV show is a typical average Nine. As a teenager, she dreams of being a princess and is not grounded in reality. She seems fragile like a Barbie doll. She has problems expressing her emotions, and when she is assertive she overdoes it. Smallville Lana Lang is one of the most frustrating Nines on television, especially since the viewers wanted her and Clark Kent (Superboy) to live happily ever after. Her eyes look dreamy, but that's because she sleepwalks through life. Lang also has a snobby edge to her, like many Nines have (and deny).

More than other Enneagram personality type, Nines usually don't have to speak much to be viewed as attractive, as well as garner sympathy. If they do speak, they are just being polite. This passive, shy, and introverted aura naturally causes people to project their own expectations on a Nine. A great example is former New York Mets pitcher Doc Gooden. Doc didn't say much and was shy to the media. As a young black NY teenager in the 1980s, the reporters created a wholesome Mr. Perfect image for him that he was unable to live up to. He crashed under the pressure of trying to live a media manufactured life. Tiger Woods is another example of the media creating an image for a Nine. The 2008 election of President Obama is more proof of this phenomena. Although Obama is more outgoing, the media still projected a messiah image onto him. This passive, receptive, somewhat blank yet "nice" image is ripe for others to transfer their own expectations and image on Nines.

For most of Smallville, Lana Lang doesn't really show the viewers why she is worthy of Clark's love. The other female character, Chloe, wants Clark much more, and does more to get his attention, and is worthy of his love, but Clark is oblivious to her feelings. Instead, Clark is obsessed with Lana. The attraction is based on Lana's physical beauty in addition to her being a laid back elusive Nine, while Chloe- we guess- is not a challenge for Clark.

Lana Lang, who tries to live a simple life, morphs into a drama queen and starts to speak up and put pressure on Clark to make a commitment. By the way, it's pretty pathetic that she has to motivate Clark. This Smallville Clark Kent is neither a Type Three (Superman) or Type Six (Kent's traditional fake personality); he's a Generation X Nine. He and Lana both can't make up their minds and seem content with dreaming about an idealistic future outside of Smallville, rather than putting together solid building blocks in the present.

Lana eventually tires of Clark's lies to cover his secret identity and becomes subconsciously attracted to Lex Luthor, although on the surface she swears it's just a friendship. You see, Nines are out of touch with their unconscious desires or deep motives. A Type Four is the master of introspection, but the Average Nine is completely clueless when it comes to being aware of her instincts.

Ask fans of Smallville about Lana Lang, and you will hear about her missed chances, hypocrisy, and even ditzy nature. Some Nines are "fashion model" types, and Lana is one, which is a shame, because Lana would have been a truly great girlfriend if she had a boyfriend who took care of her emotional needs and helped her set her future goals (and put up with her dream-like states). Lex Luthor tried this, but Lana wasn't attracted to him because he was manipulative and evil, and she still loved Clark. On the other hand, Clark held her back: a double Nine stall.

What we've learned:
- Average Nines are dreamy and fantasize about the ideal partner. They can be socially awkward, which also has an aura of snobbery.
- Some Nines are the generic "model types"- stereotypically superficial, picky drama queens.
- A double Nine relationship is sure to have romance and contentment- two "soul mates" lost in love- but may takes years (if ever) to evolve or mature into something more than a melodramatic teen romance.
- Nines are keyed into happiness through mates and environment. Unfortunately, this attachment to ideal partners or cities to live in causes them to not appreciate what they have and to grow considerably unhappy in their present.

Other Average 9's

Angel

Cursed to have his human soul trapped inside a vampire's body, forced to remember and live with his terrible actions when he was the vampire Angellus, Angel [Buffy the Vampire Slayer] attempts to make amends by fighting evil. He helped Buffy in some of her early adventures, and the two were briefly lovers. Eventually, Angel moved to Los Angeles to get away from the slayer, where he started an investigation agency to fund his efforts to battle organizations bent on destroying humanity.

Human Torch (comic book version)

Johnny Storm [Marvel Comics] is an impetuous young man whose hot-headedness matches his powers. He cares deeply for his sister, and is frequently bailed out by her and his other Fantastic Four teammates. Johnny loves to pull pranks on Ben Grimm. In the 60's, Johnny viewed Reed as a father figure. The Human Torch is all about keeping the team/family together. He is capable of falling in love and can be a committed boyfriend. Johnny has a strong 8-wing, and is a sexual subtype.

Ice

Ice [DC Comics] was a member of the Justice League International during the Keith Giffen, J.M. DeMatteis, and Kevin Macguire run in the late 1980's. An evolving character, she accidentally became the 2nd Ice Maiden due to a naming issue, and eventually became known as Ice. She is introduced as a shy, inhibited woman. Ice was dating Guy Gardner before her death, displaying patience with him that others could not. She was resurrected years later, and it was revealed that an accidental outburst of her powers, which killed her father, led to her shy demeanor. Ice has been prone to being possessed by evil doers, or lashing out without thinking.

Colossus

Raised on a farm collective in the old Soviet Union, Pietr Rasputin, a.k.a. Colossus [Marvel Comics], was recruited by Charles Xavier to be part of the new X-Men in order to rescue the old team from the mutant island Krakoa. He frequently thought of the family he left behind while with the X-Men. Colossus has a strong connection to the women in his life, including his sister Illyana, and his friend/lover Kitty Pride. A gentle giant, he rarely shows emotions, except when loved ones are in danger. Colossus only uses his mutant powers when needed, as he is afraid of hurting others.

Phoebe Halliwell

The youngest of the three Halliwell sisters, Phoebe [Charmed] constantly clashed with her oldest sister Prue, who was killed at the end of season 2 of Charmed. In season 3, she became the middle sister when a long-lost half-sister was discovered. Phoebe is known for being rebellious. She learned martial arts because her premonition witch powers seemed too passive for her. She developed more active magical powers and then was stripped of them for misusing them. Phoebe is prone to giving into temptation. There always seems to be drama in her personal life. She has had many failed relationships, including her marriage and then divorce with Cole/Balthazar. Phoebe finally settled down and married a nice cupid named Coop.

Kal-El (Man of Steel movie)

The first child born via natural methods in generations on Krypton, Kal-El was not preprogrammed to perform a specific task in life. Instead, his father Jor-El, seeking to keep Kryptonian heritage alive in the face of his planet's destruction, implanted Kal-El with the matrix used to program babies on Krypton and sent him to Earth. Kal-El grew up in Kansas as Clark Kent, adopted son of John and Martha Kent. John, fearing his son would be ostracized by society and hunted by the government, encouraged Clark to hide his powers, even chastising him when he saved lives. After wandering the country for years, anonymously rescuing people from terrible disasters, Kal-El meets a virtual representation of his father and discovers his true heritage and calling. Once he dons the suit and learns to fly, his confidence increases and he becomes Superman. He willingly turns himself over to the U.S. military when Zod threatens to destroy the Earth, and later gives himself up to Zod and his henchmen. He is willing to sacrifice his life to save humanity, even if it means turning his back completely on his Kryptonian heritage. On a personal level, he becomes protective of Lois Lane after she proves she can keep his secret, and is protective of his mother. The Man of Steel movie version of Superman has the power to permanently stop an adversary if it means saving millions of lives, and will exercise that power if necessary. The creators of the Man of Steel movie opted to focus on Kal-El's personality, and do away with the dual Clark/Superman persona of the Silver Age and Christopher Reeves Superman movies. In doing so, Clark and Superman have both become, in essence, Earthly masks for the Kryptonian Kal-El. Clark is the immature side of Kal-El, unsure of himself and his place in this world. Superman is the actualized side of Kal-El, willing to fight to save the Earth and those he loves, confident in his powers and who he is.

Barry Allen

Fear/Desires: To do his job and love his family.

Motivations: Performed heroic actions before deciding it was time to retire and build a family. Did what he had to do in order to maintain stability, including saving the universe.

Important Life Events: Marrying Iris West. Chemical accident that led to his receiving his powers. Saving the universe from destruction in Crisis of Infinite Earths.

Reactions Under Stress: A stoic, even-keeled hero who rarely puts on a display of emotion. Barry Allen shows grace under pressure.

Mental Health Range: Lives in the 1 to 3 range, except for a controversial Brad Meltzer storyline.

The Wing Slider: Slight 1-wing.

Instinctive Subtype: Self-Preservation.

Quirks: Occasionally clumsy for comedic effect. Notoriously late for everything. Recently revealed that he has a strong attachment to his mother. A great father figure role model.

Also Could Be: Due to his sacrifice in Crisis, as well as his known clumsiness and lateness, some believe Barry Allen is actually a healthy Type 6.

Barry Allen: the fastest man alive! He's DC Comics' Silver Age Flash, an iconic comic book hero. When we were originally going over the list, and when we were rereading the Flash comics from the 1980's, we had

Barry pegged as an Enneagram Type 6- the loyalist, martyr, trooper type. While doing the research for this book and revisiting those comics, we discovered the Flash is actually a Type 9.

The first hint, and in retrospect we should have gotten this at the time, was the Flash actually retired and went to live with Iris West in the 30th century. Now, how many heroes do you know who just hang up the super suit for real, for family reasons? Do you hear the crickets chirping?

Peter Parker has quit a few times, but not to settle down. He may try to convince himself that he's doing it to save Aunt May or whatever, but when Spider-man puts the costume in the garbage can and walks away down that alley in New York, muttering to himself that he quits, he's doing it out of frustration and an inability to juggle all the priorities in his life. Another example is Green Lantern. When Hal Jordan gives the ring back to the Guardians, he's not doing it for family reasons. He's doing it because he's overwhelmed with the responsibility.

When Barry Allen retired, his job was done. He wanted to live happily ever after. That is a 9 thing. He was looking at his superhero career as a job. The Flash realized that the most important thing was to live with someone whom he deeply loved and form a family with them. In order to accomplish that, he had to retire. In order to attain inner peace, and to love and be loved in a stable relationship, he had to get rid of the hectic rat race.

Another sign is that Barry Allen, after DC brought him back from the dead, is like a rock. He's like the same mood and temperament most of the time. All the other heroes look up to him because he's a very receptive, kind, gentle, stable, steady, easy-going guy. When he does get stressed out, it's not overly-dramatic, like when a 6 does it. He just is very even-keeled. You could stick a pin in him, and he wouldn't react.

Some writers try to make him a little more human, by having him get a little stressed out, such as during the new DC 52, which is a full reboot. The Barry Allen that everyone knows would act stressed out if he was late, and 9's are notorious for being late. Some 6's can tend to be late, as well, and we know that no single type owns a personality trait exclusively.

However, Barry is known for that, and so are 9's in general. It's a long-running joke that the fastest man alive is always late.

Now, another reason why one may confuse 6's and 9's is that the 6 integrates into a 9. So, a healthy 6 would act like a healthy 9. So, it's not that much of a stretch to get them confused. Therefore, you really have to look at the quirks. You have to get into their motivations, desires, and fears. You have to open the hood of the Enneagram to get to the core personality of Barry Allen.

Here's one thing: 6's are much more marketable in fiction then 9's are. That's because 6's have this whole drama thing going for them. Look at Spider-man, Green Lantern, or Frodo: you look at any of them and it's like, "Wow. People can really relate to that. People can really get into the drama and the excitement in their lives." Nines generally don't like to express their feelings, whereas 6's do tend to express them. Nines almost are enviable in that they don't blow up- especially a healthy Nine.

Barry Allen has kept his job as the police forensics technician and doesn't have a lot of different roles. He does not bounce around from job to job. That's who he is. He's the spiritual backbone of the Justice League now, since J'on J'onzz, the Martian Manhunter (another Nine), has been phased out in the new DC 52.

Here's one major quirk about Barry Allen being a 9: ever since his relaunch with Geoff Johns, they've been showing him as a sort of momma's boy. Barry Allen was totally in love with his mom. That's okay to love your mom, right? We all do, but generally, in fiction, the hero doesn't have to constantly run back to his mother. Barry Allen is really over-the-top with his mother-love in recent years.

We don't mean to say that only 9's can love their mother a lot. It's just that in the comics, she gets way too much time in his mind. Spiderman had a reason to want to protect Aunt May: because he lost Uncle Ben due to his own ignorance. Barry Allen and his mom, on the other hand? It's a Nine thing.

Another revelation: Barry Allen is a great father figure to Wally West, who was Kid Flash. After Barry Allen died by sacrificing himself in Crisis on Infinite Earths in the 1980s, Wally West assumed the mantle from Barry. He always tried to live up to Barry's great reputation. For many years, Wally West just couldn't do it. He was just constantly haunted by trying to live up to someone that was so perfect. Healthy Nines have an aura of being infallible. Not like a 1, but in a sense that they have these traits and characteristics of being patient, humble, and all-embracing. They're not trying to deceive you or hurt you. Healthy Nines are the perfect father figure type. It is a gentle type that Wally tried to copy, yet he couldn't for a long time. For years, he was struggling with that. Eventually, he found his own identity.

Ironically enough, Wally actually inspired a whole new generation of comic book readers in the 1990s. Writer Mark Waid gets full credit for that, for transforming Wally into a character that can actually, finally, move on and stop trying to live up to something that he can't. A lot of people are going to make the argument that Wally's run, pun intended, resonated more with fans than Barry ever had. After all, Barry got his comic cancelled in the 1980s. Wally West, arguably, was the most popular Flash who ever existed. That has to do with the core personality of Barry. The guy is just so even-keeled and bland that it can be a marketability problem.

Many science students and professionals like Barry because he studies physics and chemistry. He is very imaginative with the tricks he can do with his super-speed. He's not stubborn, like average 9s. He's very open-minded about using his abilities, learning about science, and teaching us, the readers, about science while he does it. Barry doesn't really have instincts for coming up with tricks to use. He has to first learn them on the job and practice it. Average Nines aren't known for instincts and getting something right the first time. In the Silver Age, Barry was shown as tripping and getting stuck in tar. He always seemed kind of detached from his instincts, which is core to Enneagram Type 9.

Even Derek Jeter, who in real life is a healthy, famous, and suave 9, was prone to errors (over 50 one season) as a young ballplayer in the minor leagues. Even now, with all his experience, there are rare times where he'll just make a boneheaded error.

One controversial storyline that the Flash was part of was written by Brad Meltzer. It was called Identity Crisis. Basically, Meltzer was showing the dark side of the DC Universe and the tough decisions heroes have to make. It really caused a storm with the fanbase at the time. A lot of fans couldn't make sense out of why their characters were acting so different, while in continuity.

Basically, the previously cheesy villain Dr. Light raped Sue Dibny, the wife of Elongated Man. The heroes voted to decide whether to mind-wipe Dr. Light, basically giving him a little lobotomy. Barry Allen voted yes, that they should do it. When Batman found out, he was against it, and they mind-wiped him, as well.

The reason given by Meltzer in the comic is that this happens six months after Iris West's death. So that is Meltzer's excuse for the Flash's behavior. It's really the only reason Barry would engage in such activity. So, let's run it through the Enneagram. Is that in character or not?

At first glance it doesn't seem proper that a moralist like Barry Allen would agree to erase memories, but when you consider that Barry's only weakness is his mother, which he transfers on to every woman he meets, and, Iris West is his number one love, then you can attempt to justify it. You can say he was not thinking clearly. He wanted to overly protect or avenge the tragedy that had befallen Sue Dibny by Dr. Light.

So, we're going to have to say, technically, Brad Meltzer was within Barry's bounds in the Enneagram, even though we feel that it is a bit of a stretch. If we were editing that comic series, we probably wouldn't have allowed it as such.

We believe people should idolize Barry Allen. He's always been on the high level of healthiness and is a wholesome moral hero.

What we've learned:
- Healthy Nines are gentle, understanding, lead by example, and are family orientated.
- Nines welcome retirement.

- Healthy Nines are drama free, which is great for real life, but somewhat boring for having a leading role in fiction.
- Healthy Nines have a strong moral compass that helps them overcome temptations.
- Nines have better control over their emotions than Sixes.

Other Healthy 9's
Luke Skywalker

Luke Skywalker [Star Wars] grew up as a farm boy on the desert planet of Tatooine. From these humble beginnings, he rose to become a leader of the Rebellion after blowing up the Death Star. His healthy desire to save his friends overruled the completion of Yoda's training program, which shows his integration to 3 when it comes to taking action. His belief that his father, Anakin Skywalker, still had good in him was so strong that he was willing to die for him.

Martian Manhunter

Extracted from Mars by Dr. Erdel's experimental beam, J'onn J'onzz [DC Comics] is one of the last living Martians. Able to shape-shift, he took on the human persona John Jones and worked as a police detective first, then a private detective. He was a founding member of the Justice League International, where he played a straight-face to the comedic antics of Booster Gold and Blue Beetle. In addition to having super-strength and the ability to fly, Martian Manhunter is a strong telepath, able to establish links between teammates during missions. Fire is his weakness, and this may be a psychological issue due to the death of his people on Mars.

Monitor

Born as a result of Krona's experiment to see the beginning of the universe, the Monitor [DC Comics] fought his antimatter counterpart until both were knocked out for billions of years. They were both awakened by another scientist. Observing the Anti-Monitor's path of destruction, the Monitor hatched a plan to test earth's heroes to find out who would be best suited to help stop his enemy and prevent the destruction of the multiverse. He planned his own death so that his powerful energies could be released, sparing Earth-1 and Earth-2 from the Anti-Monitor's anti-matter wave for a time. The Monitor was a father figure/mentor to Harbinger, whom he saved before her universe was destroyed.

Lieutenant Uhura

Nyota Uhura is primarily known by fans of Star Trek as the Communications Officer aboard the ISS Enterprise. Uhura has had multiple tours of duty on the ship, mixed in with teaching at Starfleet Academy. She has repeatedly demonstrated an ability to remain calm during tense situations, establishing communication with hostile figures from throughout the galaxy. Uhura is fun to hang out with, able to sing a song and crack jokes with her crew mates. In the latest Star Trek movies, she is in a committed relationship with Spock. Loyal to her commanding officers, she will refuse to give in to the demand of the enemy, even if it means risking injury or death. In real life, Uhura was a symbol of equality during the Civil Rights Movement, and an inspiration for a generation of minority and female NASA astronauts.

PART TEN

APPENDIX

Appendix I: List of Characters by Fictional Universe
The following is a list of the characters mentioned in this book, divided by the universe these characters exist in:

24
Jack Bauer, Type 7, Average

All in the Family
Edith Bunker, Type 2, Healthy

Buffy the Vampire Slayer
Angel, 9, Average
Buffy, Type 4, Average
Drusilla, Type 5, Unhealthy
Giles, Type 5, Healthy
Spike, Type 4, Unhealthy
The Master, Type 3, Unhealthy
Willow, Type 6, Average

Charmed
Phoebe Halliwell, Type 9, Average

DC
Anti-Monitor, Type 8, Unhealthy

Barry Allen, Type 9, Healthy
Batman, Type 7, Average
Brainiac, Type 1, Unhealthy
Captain Marvel, Type 6, Healthy
Guy Gardner, Type 8, Average
Ice, Type 9, Average
Kal-El (Man of Steel movie), Type 9, Average
Lana Lang (Smallville), Type 9, Average
Lex Luthor, Type 5, Unhealthy
Lois Lane, Type 1, Average
Martian Manhunter, Type 9, Healthy
Maxwell Lord, Type 3, Unhealthy
Monitor, Type 9, Healthy
Oliver Queen, Type 4, Average
Original Blue Beetle, Type 6, Average
Parallax, Type 6, Unhealthy
Perry White, Type 8, Average
Power Girl, Type 7, Average
Psycho Pirate, 2, Unhealthy
Regular Hal Jordan, 6, Average
Sinestro, 1, Unhealthy
Supergirl, 2, Healthy
Superman, 3, Healthy
The Joker, 6, Unhealthy
Ursa, 1, Unhealthy
Vigilante, 1, Unhealthy
Wonder Woman, 1, Healthy

Everybody Loves Raymond
Debra, 1, Average
Frank, 8, Average
Marie, 2, Unhealthy
Raymond, 1, Unhealthy
Robert, 4, Average

GI Joe
Destro, 4, Unhealthy
The Baroness, 1, Unhealthy

Godzilla
Godzilla, 8, Unhealthy

Lord of the Rings
Frodo, 6, Average

Marvel
Black Cat, 7, Average
Bruce Banner, 5, Average
Captain America, 3, Healthy
Colossus, 9, Average
Cyclops, 6, Average
Doc Samson, 5, Unhealthy
Doctor Doom, 3, Unhealthy
Hulk, 8, Unhealthy
Human Torch (comic book), 9, Average
Hyperion, 3, Average
J. Jonah Jameson, 8, Average
Loki, 5, Unhealthy
Magneto, 8, Unhealthy
Namor, 3, Average
Reed Richards, 5, Average
She-Hulk, 7, Healthy
Spider Man, 6, Average
Sue Storm, 2, Average
The Leader, 5, Unhealthy
The Thing, 7, Average
The Toad, 2, Unhealthy
The Watcher, 5, Average
Time Variance Authority, 1, Average
Tony Stark, 3, Average
Wolverine, 4, Average

Masters of the Universe
Battle-Cat, 8, Healthy
Beast Man, 2, Unhealthy
Evil-Lyn, 5, Unhealthy

He-Man, 3, Average
Man-at-Arms, 1, Average
Merman, 6, Unhealthy
She-Ra, 6, Healthy
Skeletor, 8, Unhealthy
Sorceress, 5, Healthy
Teela, 8, Average
Tri-Klops, 1, Unhealthy

Matrix
Agent Smith, 1, Unhealthy
Morpheus, 5, Healthy
Trinity, 1, Healthy

Once Upon a Time
Regina Mills, 3, Unhealthy

Robotech
Ric Hunter, 3, Healthy

Sherlock Holmes
Sherlock Holmes, 7, Average

Star Trek
Captain Kirk, 7, Average
Captain Picard, 4, Healthy
Chief Engineer Scott, 6, Average
Data, 3, Healthy
Dr. Crusher, 6, Average
Dr. McCoy, 2, Healthy
Ensign Chekov, 6, Average
Khan, 3, Unhealthy
Lt. Commander Troi, 2, Average
Lt. Uhura, 9, Healthy
Lt. Worf, 8, Healthy
Nerys Kira, 8, Average
Q, 7, Unhealthy
Quark, 8, Average

Spock, 1, Healthy
T'Pol, 1, Average
Will Ryker, 6, Healthy

Star Wars
Anakin Skywalker, 9, Unhealthy
Emperor Palpatine, 3, Unhealthy
Han Solo, 4, Average
Luke Skywalker, 8, Healthy
Padme Amidala, 1, Average
Princess Leia, 8, Average
R2D2, 2, Average
Yoda, 8, Healthy

The Fall Guy
Colt Seavers, 7, Healthy

The Incredibles
Mr. Incredible, 7, Average

The Last Airbender
Aang, 4, Average

The Office
Dwight Schrute, 5, Average

The Prisoner
Number Six, 4, Healthy

The Simpsons
Homer Simpson, 7, Average
Lisa Simpson, 4, Average

Transformers
Galvatron, 7, Unhealthy
Megatron, 8, Unhealthy
Optimus Prime, 6, Healthy

Watchmen
Dr. Manhattan, 5, Average
Nite Owl, 6, Average
Ozymandias, 3, Average
Rorschach, 4, Unhealthy

X-Files
Cigarette Smoking Man, 9, Unhealthy
Fox Mulder, 7, Average
Scully, 5, Healthy
Walter Skinner, 1, Average

Appendix II: Other Characters and Their Types

We set a hard deadline for completion of this book and decided to stick to it. As a result of this, there were many characters and universes that were left out. Rather than turn this book into an encyclopedia, we decided to stick to the over 120 examples we chose, since our goal was to use fictional characters to inform you about the Enneagram, and how it can help improve your daily life. However, there are certain to be characters that readers will be curious about. So, here is a list of additional fictional characters from worlds we like that did not get a write-up, divided by their possible personality types:

Type 1
Agent Broyles (Fringe)
Claire Underwood (House of Cards)
David Robert Jones (Fringe)
Hermione Granger (movie version)
Jerry (Seinfeld)
Ripley
Severus Snape (movie version)
Thomas Jerome Newton (Fringe)

Type 2
Elaine (Seinfeld)
Nina Sharp (Fringe)

Sam Weiss (Fringe)
Santa Claus
Sirius Black (movie version)
Tin Man

Type 3
Francis Underwood (House of Cards)
Green Goblin
Gary Mitchell (Star Trek)
John Scott (Fringe)
Olivia Dunham (alternate universe, "Faux-livia")
Peter Bishop
Voldemort (movie version)
Walternate (Fringe)

Type 4
Frankenstein's Monster (Mary Shelley book version)
Harry Potter (movie version)
Olivia Dunham
Snake Eyes
Charlie Francis (alternate universe)
Zoe Barnes (House of Cards)

Type 5
Antman
Dumbledore (movie version)
Doctor Emmett Brown
Dr. William Bell
Luna Lovegood (movie version)
Merlin
September (Fringe)

Type 6
Christina Gallagher (House of Cards)
Dr. Watson (Sir Arthur Conan Doyle book version)
Ronald Weasley (movie version)
Ensign Chekhov
Peter Bishop (original universe)

Type 7
Hercules (Marvel Comics)
Marty McFly
Kramer (Seinfeld)
Peter Russo (House of Cards)
Sarek (Star Trek)
Walter Bishop

Type 8
Archie Bunker
Bluto/Brutus
Cyrano Jones (Star Trek)
Draco Malfoy (movie version)
Frankenstein's Monster (movie versions)
Harry Mudd (Star Trek)
King Kong (original movie version)
Kronos (Wrath of the Titans)
The Spectre

Type 9
Aragorn (movie version)
Astrid (Fringe)
Charlie Francis (Fringe)
Clark Kent (Smallville TV series), 9, Average
Doug Stamper (House of Cards)
Dr. Elizabeth Dehner (Star Trek)
Gandalf (movie version)
George (Seinfeld)
Lieutenant Sulu
Neville Longbottom (movie version)

Appendix III: Changelog

Version 2013.8.26:
Rebuilt document in Scrivener due to ongoing corrupt file errors.

Version 2013.8.21:
Rebuilt previous update due to corrupted file. Corrected typo in Other Unhealthy 1's section. Corrected typo in Other Unhealthy 2's section. Corrected typo in Other Unhealthy 4's section. Added the Clark Kent (Smallville TV Series) to Appendix II. Added Kal-El (Man of Steel movie) to chapter and Appendix I.

Version 2013.8.15:
Manually corrected formatting error in Table of Contents. Added Appendix III: Changelog. Corrected typo and updated existing information in Appendix I. Updated existing information in Appendix II. Added the following characters to Appendix II: Antman, Gary Mitchell, Dr. Elizabeth Dehner, Harry Mudd, Cyrano Jones, Sarek, Lieutenant Sulu, Olivia Dunham, Agent Broyles, Charlie Francis, Astrid, David Robert Jones, Charlie Francis (alternate universe), John Scott, Nina Sharp, Olivia Dunham (alternate universe), Peter Bishop, Peter Bishop (original universe), Sam Weiss, September, Thomas Jerome Newton, Walter Bishop, Walternate, Dr. William Bell, Francis Underwood, Claire Underwood, Doug Stamper, Peter Russo, Christina Gallagher, Zoe Barnes. Added the following character summaries to the chapters and

Appendix I: Khan, Chief Engineer Scott, Colt Seavers, Lt. Uhura, Ensign Chekov, Raymond Barone, Robert Barone, Debra Barone, Marie Barone, Frank Barone.

Version 2013.4.27:

Corrected typos. Corrected listing error of some characters in Appendix 1. Revamped layout for 6" x 9" print edition of book. Reformatted the Table of Contents and added missing link. Added chapter titled, "How to Type Yourself." Updated Introduction.

Bibliography

The sources for the material in this book are too numerous to list in detail. We have done our best to reference the source material within the text of the chapters of the book. We would like to mention that *Personality Types* by Riso and Hudson was our starting point for learning about the Enneagram. *The Wisdom of the* Enneagram is also a great book for getting to know the Enneagram better.

ABOUT THE AUTHOR

Damian Hospital's writing credits include technical writing, training manuals, contracts, human resource guides, and business proposals for two IT companies. Tony Vahl is a man of mystery who has been known to podcast and blog, and is an auditor in real life.

Damian majored in Psychology in college before joining the workforce. Tony majored in Accounting.

Damian and Tony were always creative writers since grade school. They were published numerous times from then until college. In 2001, Damian and Tony co-founded news, satire, and entertainment review websites such as the DailySkew, Skew.DailySkew.com, and others.

They co-created the Dream Seeker Universe. The first short stories were published on their websites in 2001, and they continued to publish stories either on the web or via PDF downloads for years. Lulu published them in 2006, and then they realized how great the Kindle is.

CPSIA information can be obtained at www.ICGtesting.com
Printed in the USA
LVOW06s1720070214

372825LV00020B/477/P